Shakespeare for Fun

Fremdsprachentexte | Englisch

Shakespeare for Fun

Von Andrew Williams
Mit 12 Abbildungen

Reclam

Diese Ausgabe darf nur in der Bundesrepublik Deutschland,
in Österreich und in der Schweiz vertrieben werden.

This edition may only be sold in Germany, Austria and Switzerland.

RECLAMS UNIVERSAL-BIBLIOTHEK Nr. 19888
Alle Rechte vorbehalten
Copyright für diese Ausgabe
© 2014 Philipp Reclam jun. GmbH & Co. KG, Stuttgart
Gestaltung: Cornelia Feyll, Friedrich Forssman
Gesamtherstellung: Reclam, Ditzingen. Printed in Germany 2014
RECLAM, UNIVERSAL-BIBLIOTHEK und
RECLAMS UNIVERSAL-BIBLIOTHEK sind eingetragene Marken
der Philipp Reclam jun. GmbH & Co. KG, Stuttgart
ISBN 978-3-15-019888-9
www.reclam.de

Inhalt

Foreword 7

How to Spell the Name of a Well-known English Writer 11
Sobriquets

Myths about Shakespeare's Life 13
Some Things that are Actually True – "Shakespeare's Life" (Richard Armour) – Shakespeare's Pubs (Sam Schoenbaum)

Shakespeare's True Nationality 24

Shakespeare's Words 34
The Most Common Words Used by Shakespeare – Shakespeare as First User – False Friends – Where Shakespeare Got It Wrong

Insulting with Shakespeare 42
The Shakespearian Insult Generator

The Authorship Question 50
"Searching for Cyphers" (David Crystal and Ben Crystal) – "Authorship of the Plays" (Richard Armour) – "A Legendary Blues Guitarist" (Ben Crystal)

The Works 62
"William Shakespeare's Star Wars" (Ian Doescher) – "The Skinhead Hamlet" (Richard Curtis) – "The Famed 'To Be or Not To Be' Scene from Hamlet" (A modern verse rendition by Desmond Olivier Dingle) – A Soliloquy Simplified: "To Be, or the Contrary?" (Sir Arthur Quiller-Couch) – "The Tragedy of Othello" (A modern verse rendition by Desmond Olivier Dingle) – Shakespeare According to Gyles Brandreth – The Curse of Mac... – "The Macbeth Murder Mystery" (James Thurber) – "The Merchant of Venice, told by Lancelot Gobbo, Shylock's Servant" (Humphrey Carpenter) – The Sonnets – Hamlet on Film

Shakespeare – the Rude Bits 104

Performing Shakespeare 113
  "The Verse Problem – And How to Master It" (Patrick Barlow) –
  "Shakespeare Masterclass" (Stephen Fry and Hugh Laurie) –
  "A Tale of Revenge from Macbeth*" (Derek Nimmo)*

Shakespeare in the Classroom 119
  "Shakespeare's Age" (Patrick Barlow)

Cooking with Shakespeare 125
  Potage Macbethienne

Shakespeare in Advertising 130

shAkspEr 136

How to Draw Shakespeare 138

Editorische Notiz 141
Literaturhinweise 142
Text- und Abbildungsnachweise 143

Foreword

Is Shakespeare fun? Schoolchildren around the world would emphatically say: no. What is fun about reading plays that use words nobody understands anymore? What is fun about listening to teachers talk about boring topics like Elizabethan England, the War of the Roses and the iambic pentameter? Or about embarrassing topics like jealousy and homoeroticism? What is fun about being made to recite a sonnet in front of your classmates? Nothing.

On the other hand, if you ask the same schoolchildren if you can have fun *with* Shakespeare, many of them would certainly say: yes! What could be more fun than reading the whole of *Othello* in strange accents? (A favourite when I was at school was turning the Moor into an Australian.) Why not recite one of the sonnets in a monotonous voice, for example? Or what about a lisping Richard III: "Now ith the winter of our dithcontent / Made gloriouth thummer by thith thun of York." And so on and so forth.

Finding fun and hilarity where the teacher finds poetry, beauty, and human conflict, taking pleasure in ruining the texts is, of course, an act of rebellion. It is entirely understandable that schoolchildren should look for laughs this way. After all, it is very difficult indeed to get people to laugh by quoting Shakespeare at them. This is also true when performing Shakespeare. Making Shakespeare funny on stage is notoriously difficult. The great English actor

---

3 **emphatically:** nachdrücklich. | 5 **topic:** Thema. | 7 **iambic pentameter:** jambischer Pentameter (fünfhebiges Versmaß). | 9 **to recite s.th.:** etwas aufsagen, vortragen. | 16 **to lisp:** lispeln. | 19 **hilarity** [hɪˈlærəti]: Ausgelassenheit, Heiterkeit. | 26 **notoriously:** notorisch, bekanntlich.

Nigel Hawthorne has this to say about the matter: "The trouble is that the lines are little or no help, laced as they are with jokes which may have had them rolling in the aisles in Shakespeare's Day, but now fall flatter than pancakes on Shrove Tuesday."[1] And actor Antony Sher makes a similar observation about Shakespeare's clowns: "Autolycus's speeches – like all Shakespeare's clowns – are virtually incomprehensible; it's like reading a joke book in Eskimo."[2]

The fact that you cannot make anyone laugh by quoting Shakespeare at them is all the more noticeable for the fact that the opposite is true of Shakespeare's romantic poetry. How easy it is to use Shakespeare to be romantic! Simply quote a few lines from one of the sonnets: "Shall I compare thee to a summer's day?" Shakespeare is about love, after

1 Nigel Hawthorne, *Straight Face*, London: Hodder & Stoughton, 2002, p. 229.
2 Antony Sher, *Beside Myself. An Actor's Life*, London: Nick Hern Books, 2001, p. 313.

1 **Hawthorne:** Nigel H. (1929–2001), britischer Schauspieler, als eloquenter Beamter in der englischen Fernsehserie *Yes Minister* bekannt. Spielte 1995 in einer Verfilmung von *Richard III* The Duke of Clarence. | 2 **to be laced with s.th.:** mit etwas durchzogen sein. | 3 **to have s.o. rolling in the aisles:** jdn. dazu bringen, sich vor Lachen zu kugeln. | 4 **to fall flat:** nicht ankommen (Witz). | 5 **Shrove Tuesday:** letzter Tag vor dem Beginn der Fastenzeit, an dem in England traditionell Pfannkuchen gebacken werden (Faschings-, Karnevalsdienstag). | **Sher:** Antony S. (geb. 1949), aus Südafrika stammender britischer Schauspieler und Schriftsteller, bekannt für zahlreiche Auftritte mit der Royal Shakespeare Company (u. a. als Shylock, Macbeth und Malvolio); zweimal mit dem Laurence Olivier Award ausgezeichnet. | 6 **observation:** Beobachtung. | **Autolycus:** Figur aus *The Winter's Tale*. | 7f. **incomprehensible:** unverständlich. | 10 **noticeable:** bemerkbar.

all, everybody knows that. "Romeo, Romeo, wherefore art thou Romeo?" Just what kind of love Shakespeare treats in his works is a matter of debate, interpretation and speculation. Countless heterosexual couples decide to have a Shakespeare sonnet recited at their wedding, not realising that their most popular choice, sonnet 116, is almost certainly addressed by a man to a man.

And how simple it is to use Shakespeare to seem wise! Just quote Polonius' words to his son Laertes in *Hamlet*: "To thine own self be true." It doesn't really matter much that Polonius is a meddling old fool whose main aim is to stop his son having too much fun in Paris, nor that most of Shakespeare's sonnets are more intellectual than they are romantic. The effect is guaranteed nevertheless.

So, if you want to be romantic or wise, Shakespeare is your man. But if you want to make yourself sound witty or funny, then don't enlist his help. Even the hundreds (thousands?) of puns in Shakespeare's works fail to make us laugh. It all seems just a little bit too distant, too clever.

So if it seems that in *Shakespeare for Fun* we are having fun at Shakespeare's expense, that we are laughing *at* him rather than *with* him, then this is undoubtedly true, just as generations of school children have sniggered about "capering nimbly", and just as the advertising industry has

---

11 **to meddle:** sich einmischen. | 17 **to enlist s.o.'s help:** jds. Unterstützung gewinnen. | 21 **to have fun at s.o.'s expense:** auf jds. Kosten Spaß haben. | 22 **undoubtedly:** ohne Zweifel. | 23 **to snigger:** kichern. | 23 f. **capering nimbly:** »He capers nimbly in a lady's chamber / To the lascivious pleasing of a lute« heißt es vom personifizierten Krieg im ersten Monolog aus *Richard III* (I,1,13 f.) (*to caper:* lebhaft und voller Freude sein; tanzen vor Freude; *nimbly:* geschickt; *lascivious:* lüstern).

made light of Hamlet's philosophical question "To be, or not to be".

But more than that, some of the texts in *Shakespeare for Fun* also laugh at the expense of those who take Shakespeare too seriously from a scholarly perspective, and also at those from the fringe of academia who propose ludicrous theories about all sorts of aspects of his life and works. James Thurber, himself an American, makes fun of an American woman who thinks *Macbeth* is a crime story and tries to solve the mystery of Duncan's murder. Richard Armour and Woody Allen (in his text "But Soft ... Real Soft" that could not be included here) make fun of the 'authorship question', which has become an obsession in certain circles. *Shakespeare for Fun* also includes parodies of some of Shakespeare's best-known works. The English writer Richard Curtis imagines a *Skinhead Hamlet*. There are 'modern' versions of some key scenes from *Othello* and *Macbeth*. There are some absurd exam questions that will test your knowledge and try your patience.

2014 marks the 450th anniversary of Shakespeare's birth. In some way *Shakespeare for Fun* is part of these celebrations. In 2000 the *New York Times* ran a headline "At age 436, His Future Is Unlimited". We can only add, at age 450, Shakespeare's future is as unlimited as ever – as are the possibilities of having fun with him and his works.

---

1 **to make light of s.th.:** etwas bagatellisieren. | 5 **scholarly:** wissenschaftlich, gelehrt. | 6 **fringe:** Rand. | **academia** [ˌækəˈdiːmiə]: die akademische Welt. | **ludicrous** [ˈluːdɪkrəs]: lachhaft, absurd, lächerlich. | 13 **obsession:** Obsession, Besessenheit.

How to Spell the Name of a Well-known English Writer

How do you spell Shakespeare? Well, not even Shakespeare knew how to spell his own name, so it seems. We know of six signatures in Shakespeare's handwriting, including the spellings 'Shakp', 'Shaksper', 'Shakspere' and 'Shakspeare'. This may seem strange, but Shakespeare was just using the breviographic conventions of his time. In Shakespeare's time, no one really knew how to spell anything, let alone their own name.

What about Shakespeare's gravestone? Surely we can find the correct spelling there, set in stone for eternity? On the memorial plaque in the Church of the Holy Trinity, Stratford-upon-Avon, his name is spelled 'Shakspeare'. So is this the correct spelling? Well, next to this, the inscription on the grave of his widow, Anne, calls her the "wife of William Shakespeare".

And the rest of the world? How did they decide to spell Shakespeare? How have people spelled Shakespeare over the centuries? Here are some of the most popular spellings:

Schaksp.	Shake-speare	Shaksper
Shackespeare	Shakespere	Shakspere
Shackespere	Shakespheare	Shaxberd
Shackper	Shakespea	Shaxpeare
Shackspere	Shakspear	Shaxper

8 **breviographic conventions:** Schreibkonventionen, nach denen man z. B. die eigene Unterschrift, aber auch andere häufige Wörter und Ausdrücke abkürzen konnte. | 10 **let alone:** ganz abgesehen von. | 12 **set in stone:** in Stein gemeißelt. | 13 **plaque** [plaːk, plæk]: Tafel.

Shagspere	Shakspeare	Shaxspere
Shakespe	Shak-speare	Shexpere
Sakespeare		

Sobriquets

We all know that Goethe was the "Dichterfürst" (this is his 'sobriquet'), but what about Shakespeare? From very early on Shakespeare was known as the "Swan of Avon". This goes back to a poem Ben Jonson wrote for the First Folio, the first printed edition of Shakespeare's plays. It refers not only to the swans on the river of Shakespeare's birthplace, but also to the ancient belief that the souls of poets pass into swans.

Even more common than the Swan of Avon is "the Bard".

In 1769, David Garrick – an actor, writer and manager of the 18th century – called Shakespeare the bard of all bards:

The bard of all bards was a Warwickshire bard.

Today, no one ever seriously calls Shakespeare "the Bard", which is why he is referred to as the Bard throughout this book.

In conclusion: if for some reason you don't want to call Shakespeare Shakespeare, then call him the Bard, or the Swan of Avon.

---

4 **sobriquet** ['səʊbrɪkeɪ]: Spitzname. | 8 **Jonson:** Ben J. (1572–1637), englischer Dichter, *Poet Laureate* 1617. Als Mitglied von Henslowes Theatergruppe tötete er im Duell einen Schauspielerkollegen.

Myths about Shakespeare's Life

He was a deer poacher. Not long after Shakespeare's death, an obscure clergyman, Richard Davies, notes that Shakespeare was "much given to all unluckiness in stealing venison and rabbits". Furthermore, he was "oft whipped and sometimes imprisoned", which finally "made him fly his native country …"

He was a schoolmaster. Half a century after Shakespeare's death, John Aubrey reported this as fact in his *Brief Lives*.

As a young man, Shakespeare and his companions set out to the neighbouring town of Bidford to compete in a drinking competition. After being soundly defeated, Shakespeare fell asleep under a crab tree along the road. This tree, later known as Shakespeare's canopy, became a tourist attraction and was torn to bits by souvenir-hunters in 1824.

During the Lost Years, Shakespeare …

- was a conveyancer's clerk in the office of a prosperous country lawyer,
- served as a foot soldier in the campaigns in the Low Countries,
- visited Italy,
- was a teacher, or a scrivener or a gardener or a sailor or a printer or a moneylender or a coachman.

---

2 **deer:** Reh. | **poacher:** Wilderer. | 4 f. **venison:** Rehfleisch. | 13 **crab tree:** Holzapfelbaum. | 14 **canopy:** Blätterdach. | 16 **Lost Years:** Die Jahre 1585–92, in denen besonders wenig über Shakespeares Biographie bekannt ist. | 17 **conveyancer's clerk:** Notargehilfe. | **prosperous:** wohlhabend, erfolgreich. | 19 f. **Low Countries:** die Niederlande.

Shakespeare helped write the *King James Bible*. (If you look at Psalm 46 and count 46 words from the beginning, you arrive at the word 'shake'. Then if you count 46 words from the end (excluding the word 'Selah') you arrive at the word 'spear'.

When he arrived in London, he was employed at the theatre as a horse holder, according to Nicholas Rowe and Dr Samuel Johnson. In 1765, Johnson wrote that Shakespeare "was to wait at the door of the play-house, and hold the horses of those that had no servants, that they might be ready again after the performance".

Shakespeare was born in Italy and fled to England to avoid the Inquisition at age 24. There he changed his name from Michelangelo Collalanza (Italian for "shake speare") to Shakespeare.

Shakespeare smoked pot, dope, marihuana, cannabis – whatever you want to call it. South African scientists proposed that Shakespeare smoked cannabis on the basis of a misinterpretation of a phrase from sonnet number 76 ("keep invention in a noted weed") along with the discovery that pipes found in Stratford contained traces of the drug.

Prince William, Duke of Cambridge, is a direct descend-

---

1 **King James Bible:** auch *Authorized Version* genannte, 1611 erschienene, von James I. in Auftrag gegebene und von etwa fünfzig Gelehrten verfertigte Bibelübersetzung, die jahrhundertelang in vielen englischsprachigen Ländern sehr beliebt war, ohne allerdings je »autorisiert« worden zu sein. | 7 **Rowe:** Nicholas R. (1674–1718), englischer Dichter, *Poet Laureate* 1715; brachte die erste kritische Shakespeare-Ausgabe heraus (1710). | 8 **Johnson:** Dr Samuel J. (1709–84), englischer Lexikograph, Kritiker und Dichter. Bekannt vor allem für sein *Dictionary of the English Language* und seine Shakespeare-Ausgabe von 1765. | 23 f. **descendent:** Nachkomme.

ent of Shakespeare. A German scholar claimed to have found evidence that Elizabeth Vernon, who married the Earl of Southampton, was the dark lady of the Sonnets, and that Shakespeare had an illegitimate daughter by her. Since the daughter, Penelope, went on to marry the second Baron Spencer, from whom Diana Spencer was descended, this would mean that the Princes William and Harry are directly descended from Shakespeare, as is the latest addition to the Royal Family, George …

Some Things that are Actually True

- Shakespeare wasn't born on 23rd April at all. All we really know is that he was baptised in Holy Trinity Church in Stratford on 26th April. In the 18th century people decided to celebrate the 23rd April as Shakespeare's birthday – it is after all the feast day of St George, England's patron saint. But quite apart from that, 23rd April in 1564 was not the same as 23rd April today. England was still using the Julian calendar, and didn't adopt the reformed Gregorian calendar until 1752. So, in 1564, the date referred to then as 23rd April was actually the 3rd of May by today's calender.
- In celebration of Shakespeare's 400th birthday in 1964 a group of Stratford actors gave a reading in the Vatican before Pope Paul VI. They took a copy of the First Folio for His Holiness to inspect. His Holiness thought the book

15 f. **patron saint:** Schutzpatron. | 18 **Julian calendar:** im Jahr 46 v. Chr. von Julius Cäsar eingeführter Kalender (mit 365 statt wie zuvor 355 Tagen im Jahr); 1582 durch den gregorianischen Kalender abgelöst. | **to adopt:** übernehmen. | 25 **His Holiness:** Seine Heiligkeit.

was a present ... The actors were in the unfortunate position of having to correct His Holiness so they could take the valuable book back home with them.
- In 1979 India became the first country to establish a journal devoted to a single play, the twice-yearly *Hamlet Studies*.
- The Polish pianist and composer André Tchaikovsky (1935–1982) "bequeathed his skull to the Royal Shakespeare Company for use in *Hamlet*. Wrapped in a brown-paper parcel it arrived on the general manager's desk one morning along with the rest of the post."³
- Prince Charles played Macbeth at a school production in 1965.
- The smallest Shakespeare society in the world was discovered in 1888, when the journal *Shakespeariana* published a list of more than 100 Shakespeare clubs. The smallest was the "club of two", which carried on its proceedings entirely by correspondence.
- At a production of *Macbeth* in the Norwegian town of Bergen in 2001, Macbeth was represented by a tomato, Duncan by a can of tomato purée, and other leading characters by a can of beer and a thermos flask.
- At the Edinburgh Fringe Festival in 2000 Homer Simpson played Macbeth. The plot of Shakespeare's play was not changed, but the roles were taken by the cast of *The*

3 Stanley Wells, *Shakespeare: For All Time*, London: Macmillan, 2002, p. 398.

---

8 **to bequeath s.th. to s.o.:** jdm. etwas hinterlassen, vermachen. | **skull:** Schädel. | 17f. **proceedings:** Geschäfte.

Simpsons. The voices were done by the Canadian impressionist Rick Miller. Marge Simpson played Lady Macbeth, Mr Burns played Duncan, Barney played Macduff.

Is this a dagger I see before me or a pizza?
Mmmmmm ... pizza.

- In 1890, Eugene Schieffelin (1827–1906), a member of the New York Zoological Society who wanted to introduce all birds mentioned in Shakespeare's works to North America, released eighty starlings into New York's Central Park (starlings are mentioned in *Henry IV Part 1*). Before Schieffelin came along, there were no starlings in North America; now there are over 200 million of them.
- From 1990–2011 an image of Shakespeare was used for the UK's Domestic Cheque Guarantee Card scheme. The hologram, when moved from side to side, showed Shakespeare frowning, then warmly smiling.
- There are hardly any places named after Shakespeare. No town in the UK is named after him. (See, however, p. 25.)
- Ira Aldridge (1807–1893) was the first black actor to play major Shakesperian roles.
- Sarah Bernhardt (1844–1923) played the first Hamlet on film and possibly the only Hamlet with a wooden leg.
- John Barrymore (1882–1942) broke the record of 100-nights of Hamlet by performing it 101 times in 1922.

1f. **impressionist:** hier: Stimmenimitator. | 4 **dagger:** Dolch. | 9 **starling:** Star (Vogel). | 17 **to frown:** die Stirn runzeln.

- Patrick Stewart, whom many of us may know from *Star Trek*, once played a white Othello with a completely black cast.

Shakespeare's Life
by Richard Armour

William Shakespeare, later known as the Beard of Avon, was born in 1564, on April 12, 22, or 23, and all his life kept people guessing. His mother was of gentle birth, but his father, who came of yeoman stock, was born the hard way. The house in which William saw the light is much the same today as it was then, except for the admission charge.*

Shakespeare grew up in the little town of Stratford-on-Avon, learning small Latin and less Greek, according to Ben Jonson, probably because he was busy amassing the largest English vocabulary until Noah Webster. For a time he worked for his father, a glover. He was a dreamy lad, which explains the unusual number of four- and six-finger gloves

---

* Actually Shakespeare was not born in the Birthplace but in the Museum, a fact which he found embarrassing and kept secret from all but his closest friends.

---

2 **Star Trek:** etwa: »Reise durchs All«; von Gene Roddenberry (1921–91) geschaffene Fernsehserie um das Raumschiff »Enterprise« und deren Besatzung; eines der populärsten Werke in der Geschichte der Science-Fiction. | 3 **cast:** (Film-, Theater-)Besetzung. | 8 **gentle:** sanft; hier: adelig. | 9 **yeoman** ['jəʊmən]: Kleinbauer. | 10 **to see the light:** das Licht (der Welt) erblicken. | 11 **admission charge:** Eintritt(sgeld). | 14 **to amass:** anhäufen. | 15 **Webster:** Noah W. (1758–1843), amerikanischer Lexikograph; Verfasser des *American Dictionary of the English Language* (1828). | 16 **dreamy:** verträumt.

to be found in Stratford antique shops. Subsequently he was bound to a butcher, an awkward situation that kept his nose to the chopping block.

Much of his good taste Shakespeare inherited from his father, who once held the position of ale-taster for the town of Stratford. Young Will made the local team and met the Bidford Sippers in a spirited contest, winning his liter. According to Legend, the chief source of information about Shakespeare's youth, it took him two days to get home from Bidford, which was only a short walk but a long way on hands and knees.

When he was eighteen, Shakespeare met Anne Hathaway, who was eight years older and had begun to give up hope. What he saw in Anne is not known, but he may have admired her thatched roof, as so many have since. At any rate it gave him a good excuse for getting unbound from the butcher. Shakespeare's friends could see no reason for his rushing into marriage, but William and Anne could. Their daughter, Susanna, was born six months later.

Within two years, Shakespeare left for London – alone. Anne had given birth to twins, and there was no telling what she would do next. Moreover, he was accused of poaching something in a deer park, and it wasn't an egg.

Between 1585 and 1592 little is known of Shakespeare.

---

2 **to bind s.o. to s.o.:** jdn. (Lehrling) jdm. (Meister) verpflichten. |
3 **chopping block:** Hackklotz; Anspielung auf die Redewendung *to keep one's nose to the grinding stone* (auch: *grindstone*): etwa: schuften, sich dahinterklemmen. | 5 **ale-taster:** Bierkoster. | 7 **Sippers** (pl.): scherzhafter Name für die fiktive Trinkgemeinschaft (*to sip:* nippen). | **spirited:** lebendig; Wortspiel mit *spirits* ›Spirituosen‹. | 15 **thatched roof:** Reetdach. |
23 **to poach:** 1. wildern; 2. (Ei) pochieren.

These are the Lost Years, a period fraught with mystery and much more frustrating than the Lost Weekend. It may be that Shakespeare went into a deep sleep, like Rip Van Winkle, or wandered around in a daze, unaware of the execution of Mary Queen of Scots, the defeat of the Spanish Armada, and the introduction of the Irish potato. One authority, believing that Shakespeare must have been doing something of which he was ashamed, conjectures that he was a schoolteacher. This gave him access to the library, where he surreptitiously copied the plots of old plays for future use.

Some credence is given to the theory that Shakespeare during this period was holding horses outside a theater.* After eight years, he became one of the most experienced horseholders in London. It was at this time that he began to write, holding the reins in one hand and a pen in the other. His earliest history plays were on the reins of Henry VI and Richard III, internal evidence being the famous line in the latter play, "A horse! A horse! My kingdom for a horse!" a

---

* Unless they were held, they went inside to watch the play.

1 **(to be) fraught with s.th.:** voll von etwas stecken. | 2 **Lost Weekend:** Bezeichnung für einen im Suff verbrachten Zeitraum (nach dem Roman *The Lost Weekend*, 1944, des amerikanischen Schriftstellers Charles R. Jackson, 1903–1968). | 3 f. **Rip Van Winkle:** Protagonist der gleichnamigen Erzählung von Washington Irving (1783–1859), der in den Catskill Mountains (USA) einschläft und 20 Jahre später aufwacht, um eine völlig veränderte Welt vorzufinden. | 8 **to be ashamed of s.th.:** sich für etwas schämen. | **to conjecture:** mutmaßen. | 9 f. **surreptitiously** [ˌsʌrəpˈtɪʃəsli]: heimlich, verstohlen. | 11 **to give credence** [ˈkriːdəns] **to s.th.:** einer Sache Glauben schenken. | 12 **holding horses:** Wortspiel mit *to hold one's horses* ›sich selbst zügeln, sich gedulden‹. | 16 **rein:** Zügel; Wortspiel mit *reign* ›Herrschaft‹.

cry which Shakespeare must often have heard from departing theatergoers on rainy nights.

Shakespeare was very versatile. Besides being a successful playwright, he was an actor and part owner of the theater. Once when they were short of scenery he painted himself green and played a tree. When not otherwise occupied, he sold tickets at the box office and souvenir programs in the aisles. This gave rise to the theory that there were six William Shakespeares, additional evidence being the six signatures in the British Museum, each spelled a different way. But there were actually only two: the Man and the Myth.

Several times Shakespeare acted in the plays at the court of Queen Elizabeth, but the Queen was too busy watching Essex to notice. When King James came to the throne, Shakespeare was made one of the King's Men, a company of actors who had the right to protection from the King after a bad performance. Shakespeare never really excelled as an actor, but since he wrote the lines it was easy for him to learn them.

This was Merrie England, and Shakespeare had a gay time in London, his wife and children being in Stratford. He was often seen at the Mermaid Tavern, imbibing with Ben Jonson and the sons of Ben, who were sent to watch

---

3 **versatile:** vielseitig. | 7 **box office:** Theaterkasse. | 14 **Essex:** Robert Devereux, 2ⁿᵈ Earl of Essex (1566–1601), englischer Soldat und Höfling; genoss zeitweise die Gunst von Königin Elizabeth I. und warb um sie. 1601 nach diversen militärischen Fehlgriffen enthauptet. | 17 **to excel:** sich auszeichnen. | 20 **Merrie England:** Vorstellung einer typisch englischen, heilen, landwirtschaftlich geprägten Welt, die vor der industriellen Revolution existiert haben soll. Typische Symbole sind das »thatched cottage« und das »country inn«. | 22 **to imbibe** (poet.): (genüsslich und ausgiebig) trinken.

out for their father and carry him home. But his favorite pub was the Temple Bar. "Drink to me only with thine eyes," Ben was fond of saying, but Shakespeare knew he didn't mean a word of it. "O rare Ben Jonson," he would remark, clinking canikins with his friend and quaffing the good English ale.*

In his last years, having had his fun, Shakespeare returned to Stratford and lived with his wife. When he died, he bequeathed her his second-best bed, the one with the broken springs and the crack in the headboard. Who got his number one bed is a dark secret.

Over Shakespeare's grave is an inscription that says: "Curst be he that moves my bones." So far as is known, the bones have never been moved in all these years. It is possible, of course, that this book may make Shakespeare turn over in his grave, but in that case he will have moved them himself.

Shakespeare's Pubs
by Sam Schoenbaum

According to an anecdote reported by the great eighteenth-century editor Edward Capell, Shakespeare diverted him-

---

* No matter how rare Ben was to start with, by the end of the evening he was usually well done, in fact completely stewed.

---

2 f. **"Drink to me ... eyes"**: erste Zeile von Ben Jonsons Gedicht »To Celia« (1616). | 4 **rare: 1.** außergewöhnlich, hervorragend; **2.** ungegart (Bezug auf die Fußnote, Z. 23, *stewed* ›gedünstet‹, ›durch‹; ›besoffen‹). | 5 **canikin** (arch.): Becher, Trinkgefäß. | **to quaff s.th.**: etwas in sich hineinkippen. | 9 **to bequeath s.th. to s.o.**: jdm. etwas hinterlassen, vermachen. | 13 **curst**: verflucht. | 21 **to divert o.s.**: sich amüsieren.

self at an alehouse in Wincot with a fool who belonged to a neighbouring mill. Another report holds that Shakespeare often met his friends at the Greyhound in Stratford. From still a different source we learn that the Three Pigeons in Brentford was the inn favoured by Shakespeare and Jonson. The poet also frequented the Devil Tavern, presumably in London, and he sought relaxation in one of the wooden chambers of the Red Lion in the Edgware Road. On other occasions Shakespeare and his friends enjoyed their potations at on old house known as the sign of the Boar in Eastcheap. The legend to a nineteenth-century engraving of the Falcon Tavern on the Bankside informs us that this establishment was "celebrated for the daily resort of SHAKSPEARE and his Dramatic Companions". Yet another tradition maintains that the conviviality took place at a little tavern called the Globe [...]. On the road from Stratford to London, Shakespeare sometimes stopped for the night at The Olde Shippe Inne in the straggling village of Grendon Underwood, immortalized in the distich, 'Grendone Underwoode – The dirtiest towne that ever stood'; in the nineteenth century, visitors would be escorted up the old oak staircase, with its quaint balustrades, to the gabled third storey, where in a room with a curious little oval window the great man had slept.

---

1 **alehouse:** Wirtschaft, Lokal. | 9 f. **potations** (poet., iron.): Getränke. | 11 **engraving:** (Kunst-)Stich. | 13 **resort:** Zuflucht(sort). | 15 **conviviality:** Gesellschaft. | 18 **to straggle:** verstreut liegen. | 19 **distich** ['dɪstɪk]: Distichon (Zweizeiler). | 21 **to escort s.o.:** jdn. begleiten. | 22 **quaint:** urig, entzückend. | **balustrade:** Geländer. | **gabled:** gegiebelt. | 23 **storey:** Stockwerk.

Shakespeare's True Nationality

Shakespeare was German. It is true that he was *born* in England, but the more you think about it, the more likely it seems that Shakespeare was actually German. To be more precise: the more the *Germans* thought about it, the more certain *they were* that Shakespeare was German.

This sounds confusing, but it is really quite simple. We could start with a simple fact: Shakespeare is better in German. Germans experience the poetry and drama of Shakespeare without having to worry about all those difficult words Shakespeare used. Who cares about the occasional inevitable inaccuracies of any translation? Who cares if the puns don't work (they aren't really very funny or poetic anyway). What really matters is drama and poetry. And it is here that Germans have such a great advantage over people who don't speak or understand German. Germans experience Shakespeare more directly than we English speakers ever will.

'Shakespeare in German' is not just an English writer whose plays work well in another language. Shakespeare in German is *a major German playwright*! He is a German classic. Goethe, Schiller, Shakespeare. These are the great literary icons of German culture.

The first people to realise that Shakespeare was German were, of course, the Germans – we are not talking about any old Germans, these people were serious German philosophers and philologists. People like August Wilhelm Schlegel, who said Shakespeare is "completely ours". From

---

12 **inevitable:** unvermeidlich. | **inaccuracy** [in'ækjərəsi]: Ungenauigkeit.

A Shakespearean Map of the U.S.A.

featuring towns that actually exist!

around the mid-18th century the first good Shakespeare translations began to appear. The upsurge in nationalism coincided with the work of Wieland, Schlegel and Tieck. A steady procession of heavy-weight German poets and artists spent so much time thinking about Shakespeare and his works, on the one hand, and about their own nation, Germany, (which didn't really exist in any entirely satisfactory way), on the other, that the connection between Germany and Shakespeare became clearer and clearer. Shakespeare was seen as an example to follow for the creation of a national literature. Shakespeare became an effective propaganda tool for the cause of German nationalism.

The Germans, as a sign of their seriousness, founded the world's first academic Shakespeare society in 1864 (it still organizes an annual conference). Since then, the Germans have been taking Shakespeare very seriously. Indeed, the *Shakespeare-Jahrbuch* is the oldest Shakespeare periodical still existing. The *Shakespeare-Gesellschaft* wasn't just any old literary society with a few members here and there who had nothing better to do: in 1911 it was so well-respected that it counted not only the Emperors of Germany and Austria, but also the King of England and the US President, Theodore Roosevelt among its members.

The *Shakespeare-Gesellschaft* was dedicated to working on Shakespeare. And the more work the Germans did on Shakespeare, the more obvious it became that he was theirs. Gerhart Hauptmann hit the nail on the head when he gave a speech before the society in 1915:

2 **upsurge:** rasche Zunahme. | 3 **to coincide with s.th.:** mit etwas (zeitlich) zusammenfallen. | 7 **satisfactory:** zufriedenstellend. | 24 **to be dedicated to s.th.:** einer Sache verschrieben sein.

> Es gibt kein Volk, auch das englische nicht, das sich ein Anrecht wie das deutsche auf Shakespeare erworben hätte. Shakespeares Gestalten sind ein Teil unserer Welt, seine Seele ist eins mit unserer geworden; und wenn er in England geboren und begraben ist, so ist Deutschland das Land, wo er wahrhaft lebt.⁴

This was in 1915. Just one year later, Shakespeare had become the topic of speculation, as Germans thought about the prospect of not simply saying Shakespeare was German in a metaphysical sense, but of actually taking possession of him in accordance with international law:

> […] falls es uns glückt, England niederzuzwingen, dann meine ich, wir sollten in den Friedensvertrag eine Klausel setzen, wonach William Shakespeare auch formell an Deutschland abzutreten ist. Ich glaube sogar, für diese Abtretung werden die Engländer noch am ehesten zu haben sein, weil sie ohnehin nichts Rechtes mit ihm anzufangen wissen.⁵

That is how Ludwig Fulda put it, a German poet and playwright who has proven that if you want to be remembered,

---

4 Gerhart Hauptmann, "Shakespeare und Deutschland", in: *Shakespeare-Jahrbuch* 51 (1915) p. xiii – Mit freundlicher Genehmigung von Anja Hauptmann, Berlin.

5 Ludwig Fulda, *Deutsche Kultur und Ausländerei*, Leipzig 1916, p. 13 f. (Zwischen Krieg und Frieden, vol. 31).

---

9 **prospect of:** Aussicht auf. | 10 f. **to take possession of s.th.:** etwas in Besitz nehmen. | 11 **in accordance with international law:** gemäß internationalem Recht.

you just have to say something absurd in public, preferably in writing. And Fulda was quite right. The English had no idea what to do with Shakespeare. For centuries they had been struggling to come to terms with him. They had given his plays happy endings, they had made fun of him, and above all, they had failed to do any significant work on him. What a stroke of luck that the Germans were so industrious.

In the words of Leo Tolstoy: Shakespeare's "fame originated in Germany, and thence was transferred to England."[6] The Irish writer George Bernard Shaw suggested that the 300th anniversary of Shakespeare's death (in 1916) should be celebrated in Berlin (this may have something to do with the fact that Shaw himself was not a big fan of Shakespeare – maybe he just wanted to be as far away from the celebrations as possible).

According to one German:

> Wir haben ein unzweifelhaftes R e c h t, Shakespeare als den u n s r i g e n anzusehen, weil wir ihn durch deutschen Fleiß, deutschen Geist und deutsche Wissenschaft dazu gemacht haben.[7]

---

6 Quoted in: Werner Habicht, "Shakespeare in Nineteenth-Century Germany: The Making of a Myth", in: *Nineteenth-Century Germany. A Symposium*, edited by Modris Eksteins and Hildegard Hammerschmidt, Tübingen: Gunter Narr, 1983, p. 141.

7 Karl Fulda, *William Shakespeare. Eine neue Studie über sein Leben und Dichten*, Marburg: Oskar Ehrhardt's Universitäts-Buchhandlung, 1875, p. 125 f.

---

4 **to come to terms with s.th.:** sich mit etwas arrangieren, abfinden. |
7 f. **industrious:** fleißig.

This means Homer was also German, as were most of the ancient Greek poets and writers, who were, after all, also subject to German industry, spirit and scholarship. In fact, Troy, which was excavated by the German archaeologist Heinrich Schliemann, is essentially a German city.

The First World War put German Shakespeare admirers in a difficult position, but they still had no difficulty, for example, exhorting the German troops to success by quoting from *Henry V*: "Oh God of battles, steel my soldiers' hearts" (IV,1,286). Shakespeare was seen as part of Germany's "spiritual armament". And during the 1920s things became even more complex. Some Germans showed themselves to be very progressive, using *Hamlet* to make a political statement about the rottenness of the emerging Nazi ideology, and putting on some of the earliest 'modern-dress' productions, much to the horror of Nazi thugs and their reactionary aesthetic.

Why *did* the Nazis like Shakespeare so much that they wanted to 'protect' him? The answer is quite simple: he was not Jewish, and he did not propagate too many notions of Humanity. There are plenty of heroic deeds in his plays (certainly many more than in all of Goethe, where there is too much philosophising going on), and a good deal of violence and murder. In general, the more brutal and violent a play, the more the Nazis liked it. This made him a much

---

3 **to be subject to s.th.:** einer Sache ausgesetzt sein; Gegenstand von etwas (z. B. einer bestimmten Tätigkeit) sein. | **industry:** hier: Fleiß. | 4 **to excavate:** ausgraben. | 5 **essentially:** im wesentlichen. | 8 **to exhort:** ermahnen, antreiben. | 11 **armament:** Bewaffnung. | 14 **rottenness:** Fäulnis. | 16 **thug:** Rüpel. | 20 **to propagate s.th.:** etwas verbreiten. | **notion:** Vorstellung.

better choice during Germany's darkest years than, say, Lessing or even Schiller, even though some Germans thought he was a Nazi.[8] *Hamlet* gained a special significance. Germans saw Hamlet as one side of their national character (the other was Faust). In the 19th century Ferdinand Freiligrath had proclaimed

> Deutschland ist Hamlet
> Ernst und stumm ...

Hamlet was seen as the prototype of the intellectual, the thinker who places words before action and is too busy thinking about freedom to take part in the revolution. By the time the Nazis took power, it was time for a calculating, avenging hero. A mean Hamlet. A Hamlet who takes no prisoners and who knows what he wants. Hamlet was turned into a Germanic Hero. Joseph Goebbels' propaganda ministry actually produced a re-written version of *Hamlet*. They removed all his hesitations, his doubts and turned him into a blue-eyed blonde man of action; a soldier wrote home from the front in 1941:

[8] Schiller, by the way, translated *Macbeth* into German. He turned the witches into classical furies and left out some of the offensive and vulgar bits. In other words, he completely misunderstood the play.

> Hamlet ist weder Engländer noch Däne, er ist der germanische, wir dürfen heute sagen: Deutsche Denker, Dichter, Träumer, und in jedem Sinn Kämpfer.[9]

Adolf Hitler himself was as fond of Shakespeare as your average Nazi, but he couldn't stand Hamlet. Hamlet probably wouldn't have liked Hitler much either.

But enough history! Let's see if Shakespeare really *is* better in German. It goes without saying that the title of *The Merchant of Venice* is much better in German: *Das Kaufhaus von Venedig*. But what about the poetry of Shakespeare, his language and imagery? Is "Sein oder Nichtsein" really better than "To be, or not to be"? Doesn't that mean "Being or Not-Being?" The Germans are being far too philosophical here.

If Hamlet was Germanic, then we could also say that *Macbeth* is not set in Scotland, but rather in the Bavarian Alps, where the witches say not "Fair is foul, and foul is fair" but "Schee is schiach und schiach is schee!"[10] And so we can conclude by saying "The bard of all bards was a Bavarian bard" (see p. 12).

Here are two examples to prove it:

9 Rudolf Huch, *William Shakespeare. Eine Studie*, Hamburg: Hanseatische Verlagsanstalt, 1941, p. 91.
10 Johannes Reitmeier in: Wolfgang Weiß, *Shakespeare in Bayern – und auf Bairisch*, Passau: Karl Stutz, 2008, p. 186.

---

5 **not to be able to stand s.o.:** jdn. nicht ausstehen können. | 8 **It goes without saying:** Es erübrigt sich zu sagen.

Sonnet 18 in Bavarian
   by Jürgen Gutsch

Mei Deanei is vui scheena wiara Föhndog,
gar net so wuid wia's Weda, moanat i!
Glaabst, dass i bei de Bleaman ebba sehng mog,
wann s' in an Hagel zaust wean? No waarn s' hi!
Boi oans in dera Hitzn schnaufat, schwitzat,
waar so vui krachats Liacht gor nimma schee,
un was ko meara laichten, boi's scho blitzat,
des is dem Weda grad sei oida Schmäh.
Jatz du, mei Liawe! Ewig schaugst du drei no,
so liab un jung, so sauber und so frisch!
Da Boandlkramer woaß, du weast di sei do
in dausent Johr net! Naa, an insan Disch
   sing i un schpui vo dir, und sog's an jedn,
   un du bist oiwei do, bloß zweng mein Redn!

"All the world's a stage" in Bavarian
   by Hanns Vogel

   A Theater is as ganze Lebn,
   An jedm is sei Rolln drinn gebn.
   Siebn Akt lang dauert oft des Spui,
   Und manchmal werd de Sach oam z'vui:

I. Akt   As Butzerl, dees im Wagerl kraht,
         Is froh, daß mas net abtriebn hat.

---

17 **All the world's a stage:** *As You Like It* II,7,139 (vgl. S. 134f.).

II. Akt   Der Hundsbua, der mim Mofa karrt,
          Wia nomal wuid am Fuaßweg fahrt.

III. Akt Der Twen, der d'Madln richti pflanzt,
          Wia damisch in der Disco tanzt.

IV. Akt   Drauf als Soldat der Bundeswehr
          Lernst schiaßn du net bloß mim Gwehr.
          Sunst kimmst halt im Zivildienst dro;
          Du suachst als armer Sani-Mo
          Mit Protestiern an wahrn Friedn
          Im ausglaartn Botschamberl drinn.

V. Akt   Und bringst as bis zum Richter nauf,
          Hängst d'Welt am Paragraphn auf.
          So werst im Urteiln niamals müad,
          Daß ja koam Strizzi was passiert.

VI. Akt   Bald scho an alter Krautrer werst,
          Wos d' na in a Spital neighörst.
          Allmähli gehst aa ziemli krumm.
          Na setzns dir im Klinikum
          A ganz neus künstlichs Hüftglenk ei;
          Dees tuat jetza so Mode sei.

VII. Akt Am End konnst schier gar nix mehr sehng,
          Dei Bruinglasl tuast oft verlegn.
          Doch dees is halt as Allerschlimma:
          Der beste Schweinsbrat'n schmeckt dir nimma.
          Der Kranknschein dei Lebn begleit,
          Beim Dokter bist de mehra Zeit
          's Gebiß halt kaam mehr drin im Mäu.
          Der Vorhang fallt, na is' vorbei.

Shakespeare's True Nationality   33

Shakespeare's Words

At last, modern computer technology has made it possible to do a complete survey of Shakespeare's works to answer one of the most pressing questions of Shakespeare scholarship: Which words did the greatest poet ever to have lived use most often? Which words from his enormous vocabulary did he particularly favour? Here are the astonishing results.

The Most Common Words Used by Shakespeare

1. the
2. and
3. I
4. to
5. of
6. a
7. you
8. my
9. that
10. in
11. is
12. not
13. with
14. for
15. it
16. me
17. his
18. be

Shakespeare as First User

A search of the Oxford English Dictionary will reveal that Shakespeare is recorded as the first person to use a word in over 1500 cases. Often he used a word in a new way, for example by using a verb as a noun, or (more commonly) a noun as a verb (something linguists call *word-class conversion*, or *functional shift*). He does this with names:

---

3 **survey:** Untersuchung. | 4 **pressing:** dringend. | 7 **to favour:** bevorzugen.

> Petruchio is *Kated* [has been treated like Kate]
> *The Taming of the Shrew* III,2,244

He does it with parts of the body:

> *arm* him [give him arms]
> *Cymbeline* IV,2,400

> such stuff as madmen *tongue* [say]
> *Cymbeline* V,4,147

> I *eared* her language [listened to]
> *The Two Noble Kinsmen* III,1,29

And he does it with abstract concepts:

> can you hear a good man groan / And ... not *compassion* him? [have compassion with]
> *Titus Andronicus* IV,1,123

Here are some more words Shakespeare 'invented' – they were first recorded in his works.

alarmed	elbow	mountaineer
amazing	excitement	opulency
assassination	eyeball	puppy-dog
birthplace	fairyland	skim-milk
compassion	fashionable	undress
contaminated	gossip	upstairs
dawn	lonely	useful
delighted	moonbeam	useless

Shakespeare's Words   35

False Friends

Reading Shakespeare is difficult. One reason he is difficult is the fact that there are lots of words in his plays that people don't use anymore, such as 'gabardine', 'gaskins' and 'guerdon'. But not only that, words you think you understand might actually mean something completely different. For native speakers, reading Shakespeare can be like reading another language, complete with the so-called 'false friends'. Here are just a few of them.

awful

If something is awful, then it is very bad (awful wine, awful food at an awful restaurant), but in Shakespeare it is awe-inspiring, or worthy of respect. In *The Two Gentlemen of Verona* one of the outlaws remarks that they have been "Thrust from the company of awful men" (IV,1,44). This means that they have unwillingly left the company of men whom they respect – in other words they are social outcasts.

bootless

If we are 'bootless' then we are without boots (this, admittedly, is a word you will hardly ever use, indeed that probably has hardly *ever* been used). But in Shakespeare it means 'fruitless, useless':

---

12 f. **awe-inspiring:** Ehrfurcht gebietend.

> [...] as I have seen a swan
> With bootless labour swim against the tide
> And spend her strength with over-matching waves.
> *3 Henry VI*, I,4,20–22

If the swan had been wearing boots, one might add, swimming against the tide would have been even more difficult.

bully

We all know what a bully is: a tyrannical coward who terrorizes the weak. But in Shakespeare it is a dear friend or even a sweetheart. Shakespeare usually uses this simply as an addition to a name, as in the following examples:

> God bless thee, bully doctor.
> *The Merry Wives of Windsor* II,3,17

> O sweet bully Bottom!
> *A Midsummer Night's Dream* IV,2,18

doubt

If we doubt something, then we are uncertain whether it is true, or we hesitate to believe it. In Elizabethan times, to doubt something meant to fear it. Saying "it is to be doubted" meant 'it is to be feared'. There is a good example in *Macbeth* (IV,2,67):

> I doubt some danger does approach you nearly.

---

8 **coward**: Feigling. | 18 **to hesitate**: zögern, zaudern.

Shakespeare's Words

These are the words of a messenger who is concerned for the safety of Macduff's family. His words are not meant to make Lady Macduff feel better, but rather to warn her of an imminent danger: shortly after, Lady Macduff and her children are murdered.

nice

Today, 'nice' is one of the most overused words in the English language. "Nice weather", "nice people", "nice cake", "nice colleagues" and so on. Or you can just say "nice"' to mean 'I like it', 'I liked it', or even 'that sounds good'. In Shakespeare, nice has many more meanings. Here are some of them:

- *lustful:* "nice wenches" (*Love's Labour's Lost* III,1,21).
- *fastidious:* In *Henry V*, Henry talks to Katherine about the "nice fashion" (V,2,272) in her country. He is not paying her a compliment; he is saying that he thinks French conventions are too fussy and complicated.
- *trivial:* In *Romeo and Juliet*, Benvolio describes the quarrel between Romeo and Tybalt as "nice" (III,1,153).
- *skilful:* In *Much Ado About Nothing* (V,1,75) Leonato talks about Claudio's "nice fence". He is not referring to his attractive garden, but to his fencing skills.

quick

If we are quick, then we are speedy and fast. In Elizabethan English it can mean 'living', or 'full of life'.

4 **imminent danger:** drohende Gefahr. | 13 **lustful:** lüstern. | **wench:** Dirne. | 14 **fastidious:** anspruchsvoll, pingelig. | 17 **fussy:** pingelig. | 20 **skilful:** geschickt. | 22 **fencing:** Fechten.

When Laertes tells everyone to "pile your dust upon the quick and the dead" at the end of *Hamlet* (V,1,247), he means simply the 'living and the dead'.

revolve

If something revolves, then it makes a circular motion, but when Shakespeare's figures say 'revolve', they mean to consider, ponder, or meditate. "And you may then revolve what tales I have told you" (*Cymbeline* III,3,14).

rude

We speak of rude behaviour, or a rude gesture, but in Shakespeare "rude" means 'violent', 'ignorant' or 'uncultured'. Puck calls the rustics "rude mechanicals" in *A Midsummer Night's Dream* III,2,9; the "rough rude sea" in *Richard II* (III,2,50) is the 'rough stormy sea'; and Richard the Third laments in his opening monologue that he is "rudely stamped" (I,1,16), meaning he is imperfectly formed.

safe

If we are safe, we are not in danger. In Shakespeare it can mean 'certain' or 'sure'. When Macbeth asks: "But Banquo's safe?" (III,4,24), he does not want to know whether Banquo is in safety. Quite the opposite. He wants confirmation that the murderers have killed Banquo, that Banquo is certainly dead.

---

7 **to ponder:** nachdenken, grübeln, abwägen. | 12 **rustic:** Bauer. | 15 **to lament:** beklagen.

want

If we want something we wish or desire it, or we need it. In Shakespeare's English 'want' means to be without something. "Now I want / Spirits to enforce, art to enchant", remarks Prospero in the epilogue to *The Tempest* (line 14).

Where Shakespeare Got It Wrong

- Shakespeare got it wrong when he mentioned the game of billiards in *Antony and Cleopatra* (II,5,3). Billiards wasn't invented until the late Middle Ages.
- Shakespeare also got it wrong when he has Cassius say "The clock hath stricken three" (*Julius Caesar* II,1,192). Mechanical clocks weren't invented until the early fourteenth century.
- And Shakespeare got it wrong when Gloucester mentions "spectacles" in *King Lear* (I,2,36). There were no spectacles in ancient Britain. Gloucester would have had to wait until the thirteenth century to get some – and even then he wouldn't have found any in Britain. They were invented in Italy.
- Shakespeare got it wrong when he says that Hamlet, who lived in the twelfth century, studied in Wittenberg (I,2,113). There was no university in Wittenberg until 1502.
- And, finally, Shakespeare got it wrong in *Troilus and Cressida* II,2,165 when he has Hector, who was involved in the Trojan War (which took place in the 13th century BC), refer to Aristotle, who wrote his works nine hundred years later.

15 **spectacles** (pl., poet.): Brille.

Shakespeare was a dramatist of note;
He lived by writing things to quote.[11]

11 V. Hugo Dusenbury [Pseudonym of Henry Cuyler Bunner], "Shake, Mulleary and Go-ethe", in: *Puck* 6,151 (28 January 1880) p. 762.

[Abbildung] **Brevity is the soul of wit:** *Hamlet* II,2,90.

Insulting with Shakespeare

Modern insults have become very boring indeed. Try some of these instead:

> I do desire we may be better strangers.
> *As You Like It* III,2,253

> He is deformèd, crookèd, old and sere,
> Ill-faced, worse-bodied, shapeless everywhere,
> Vicious, ungentle, foolish, blunt, unkind,
> Stigmatical in making, worse in mind.
> *The Comedy of Errors* IV,2,19–22

> Thou whoreson, senseless villain!
> *The Comedy of Errors* IV,4,25

> Dissembling harlot, thou art false in all!
> *The Comedy of Errors* IV,4,102

> More of your conversation would infect my brain.
> *Coriolanus* II,1,92

> The tartness of his face sours ripe grapes.
> *Coriolanus* V,4,17 f.

---

4 **desire:** Begierde. | 6 **sere** [sɪəʳ]: trocken, verdorrt. | 8 **blunt:** dumm. | 9 **stigmatical:** entstellt, hässlich. | 11 **whoreson:** Hurensohn. | **villain:** Schurke, Bösewicht. | 13 **dissembling:** falsch, betrügerisch. | **harlot:** Metze, Dirne, Hure. | 17 **tartness:** Säure; Säuerlichkeit. | **to sour s.th.:** etwas sauer machen, säuern.

Away. Thou'rt poison to my blood.
Cymbeline I,1,128 f.

O thou vile one!
Cymbeline I,1,143

They have a plentiful lack of wit.
Hamlet II,2,202

This sanguine coward, this bed-presser, this horseback-breaker, this huge hill of flesh!
1 Henry IV II,5,245–247

'Sblood, you starveling, you elf-skin, you dried neat's tongue, you bull's pizzle, you stock-fish! – O, for breath to utter what is like thee! – you tailor's-yard, you sheath, you bow-case, you vile standingtuck!
1 Henry IV II,5,248 f.

There's no more faith in thee than in a stewed prune.
1 Henry IV III,3,112

---

3 **vile:** gemein, niederträchtig, abscheulich. | 5 **plentiful:** reichlich. | 7 **sanguine:** blutrot. | 10 **'Sblood:** Fluch (aus: *God's Blood*). | **starveling:** Hungerleider, abgemagertes Wesen. | 10 f. **neat's tongue:** Ochsenzunge. | 11 **pizzle:** Penis. | 12 **to utter:** äußern. | 12 f. Die folgenden Begriffe **tailor's-yard** (langer Stock zum Abmessen von Stoffen), **sheath** (Schwertscheide), **bow-case** (Behälter für einen Bogen) und **standingtuck** (*tuck:* langes, dünnes Schwert) sollen alle die Schwäche und wenig imposante Erscheinung des Beleidigten veranschaulichen. | 15 **stewed prune:** wörtl.: gedünstete Backpflaume; (slang, arch.) Prostituierte, Hure.

Away, you mouldy rogue, away!
2 Henry IV II,4,121

Away, you cutpurse rascal, you filthy bung, away! By this wine, I'll thrust my knife in your mouldy chaps an you play the saucy cuttle with me! Away, you bottle-ale rascal, you basket-hilt stale juggler, you!
2 Henry IV II,4,124–128

O braggart vile, and damnèd furious wight!
Henry V II,1,58

Avaunt, you cullions!
Henry V III,2,22

He is white-livered and red-faced.
Henry V III,2,33

Hag of all despite!
1 Henry VI III,5,12

Thou misshapen dick!
3 Henry VI V,5,35

---

1 **mouldy:** verschimmelt. | 3 **cutpurse:** Taschendieb. | **bung:** Taschendieb; Propfen (Penis). | 4 **chaps** (pl.): Kiefer. | **an:** hier: *if.* | 5 **saucy:** frech, unverschämt. | **cuttle:** hitziger Rüpel. | 6 **basket-hilt stale juggler:** etwa: lahmer Korbschwert-Jonglierer, d. h. ungeschickter Fechter. | 8 **braggart:** eitler Angeber. | **furious:** leidenschaftlich, reizbar. | **wight** (arch.): Person, Mensch. | 10 **avaunt** (arch.): hinweg! | **cullion:** Schweinehund, Mistkerl. | 12 **white-livered:** feige, schwach. | 14 **hag:** Hexe, bösartige Fee. | 16 **dick:** etwa: niedriger, kleinlicher Beamter.

44 Insulting with Shakespeare

You blocks, you stones, you worse than senseless things!
Julius Caesar I,1,35

A knave, a rascal, an eater of broken meats, a base, proud, shallow, beggarly, three-suited, hundred-pound, filthy worsted-stocking knave; a lily-livered, action-taking, whoreson, glass-gazing, super-serviceable, finical rogue; one-trunk-inheriting slave; one that wouldst be a bawd in way of good service, and art nothing but the composition of a knave, beggar, coward, pander, and the son and heir of a mongrel bitch, one whom I will beat into clamorous whining if thou deniest the least syllable of thy addition.
King Lear II,2,13–22

Thou whoreson Z, thou unnecessary letter!
King Lear II,2,62

Out, dunghill!
King John IV,3,87

---

3 **knave** [neɪv]: Knabe; Schlingel, Schurke. | **broken meats:** Fleischreste. | **base:** unehrenhaft, niedrig. | 4 **beggarly:** verarmt, mittellos. | 5 **worsted-stocking:** (im Vergleich zu Seide minderwertiger) Wollstrumpf. | **lily-livered:** feige, schwach. | 6 **finical:** pingelig, kleinlich. | **rogue:** Spitzbube. | 7 **one-trunk-inheriting:** etwa: bettelarm (denn alles, was er erben wird, passt in einen einzigen Koffer). | **bawd:** Zuhälter, Kuppler. | 9 **coward:** Feigling. | **pander:** Zuhälter, Kuppler. | 10 **mongrel bitch:** Mischlingshündin. | 10 f. **clamorous** [ˈklæmərəs]: lärmend. | 11 **to whine:** jaulen, heulen. | 16 **dunghill:** Misthaufen.

You are a tedious fool.
Measure for Measure II,1,112

Some report a sea-maid spawned him, some that he was begot between two stockfishes. But it is certain that when he makes water his urine is congealed ice.
Measure for Measure III,1,372–374

A very scurvy fellow.
Measure for Measure V,1,136

Thou art a Castalian King Urinal!
The Merry Wives of Windsor II,3,31

You juggler, you canker-blossom!
A Midsummer Night's Dream III,2,283

My cousin's a fool, and thou art another.
Much Ado About Nothing III,4,10

Thou lump of foul deformity!
Richard III I,2,57

Thou [art] unfit for any place but hell.
Richard III I,2,109

---

1 **tedious:** langweilig, langwierig und daher anstrengend. | 3 **to spawn:** laichen. | 4 **to beget:** zeugen. | 5 **congealed:** eisig, gefrierend. | 7 **scurvy:** verachtenswert. | 9 **urinal:** Urinflasche. | 11 **canker:** Geschwür. | **blossom:** Blüte. | 15 **deformity:** Missbildung.

Out of my sight! Thou dost infect my eyes.
Richard III I,2,148

A knot you are of damnèd bloodsuckers.
Richard III III,3,5

You peasant swain, you whoreson, malthorse drudge!
The Taming of the Shrew IV,1,115

Thou bitch-wolf's son!
Troilus and Cressida II,1,10

Thou stool for a witch!
Troilus and Cressida II,1,43

Thou sodden-witted lord, thou hast no more brain than I have in mine elbows.
Troilus and Cressida II,1,44f.

---

1 **thou dost:** *you do.* | 5 **peasant:** Bauer. | **swain:** (verachtenswerter) Hinterwäldler, Kerl. | **malthorse:** starkes Brauereipferd; (fig.) Arbeiter, Trottel. | **drudge:** Knecht, Arbeitstier. | 11 **sodden-witted:** (wegen übermäßigen Alkoholkonsums) schwachsinnig (*sodden:* durchweicht).

The Shakesperian Insult Generator

Simply choose one word from each column, examine them closely so you have an idea how to pronounce them, take a deep breath, and shout:

THOU ...

bawdy	bat-fowling	barnacle!
beslubbering	beef-witted	boar-pig!
bootless	beetle-headed	bugbear!
frothy	boil-brained	bum-baily!
impertinent	clay-brained	clack-dish!
lumpish	dizzy-eyed	clotpole!
mammering	fen-sucked	flap-dragon!
pribbling	flap-mouthed	foot-licker!
puny	fly-bitten	gudgeon!
saucy	folly-fallen	hugger-mugger!
spleeny	guts-griping	maggot-pie!
spongy	knotty-pated	malt-worm!
tottering	milk-livered	measle!
unmuzzled	onion-eyed	nut-hook!
weedy	plume-plucked	puttock!
fusty	swag-bellied	strumpet!
wimpled	tickle-brained	wagtail!
burly-boned	toad-spotted	popinjay!
odiferous	malmsey-nosed	scullian!
fishified	unwash'd	toad!

The Authorship Question

> I know not whether Bacon wrote the works of Shakespeare, but if he did not, it seems to me he missed the opportunity of his life.
> J.M. Barrie

For some reason, many people do not believe that Shakespeare wrote his own plays. The search for the real author of the plays shows no sign of ending. There have been many candidates for the authorship of Shakespeare's plays. The list includes Ben Jonson, Christopher Marlowe, the Earl of Derby, the Earl of Rutland, the Earl of Southampton, the Earl of Essex, Sir Walter Raleigh, Francis Bacon, Queen Elizabeth I, King James, El Spar (an Arab sheik), Edward DeVere (the 17th Earl of Oxford) and Daniel Defoe. Each theory has its congregation of true believers. And when we say 'true believers' we mean it. Let's take Daniel Defoe as an example. Now, Defoe wasn't born until 1660, and yet, according to the so-called "Defoe theory" he wrote plays that were first performed some 60 years earlier. A true believer doesn't let a small detail like that get in the way of things.

Most work has been done pursuing the theory that Francis Bacon (1561–1626) wrote Shakespeare's plays. In the 1840s, Delia Bacon (1811–1859), an American, became convinced that Shakespeare was not the author of his own

---

5 **Barrie:** James Matthew B. (1860–1937), schottischer Schriftsteller. Berühmt ist sein Kinderbuch *Peter Pan* (1904). | 15 **congregation:** Gemeinde. | **true believers:** überzeugte Anhänger. | 22 **to pursue s.th.:** etwas (weiter)verfolgen, einer Sache nachgehen.

plays;[12] and she became equally convinced that she was doing God's work by showing the world that Francis Bacon was the true author. She did God's work in an article, "Shakespeare and His Plays: An Inquiry Concerning Them" and in an unread – and unreadable – book, *The Philosophy of the Plays of Shakespeare Unfolded*. After travelling to England, where she attempted to open Shakespeare's grave, she went mad and died in an institution in 1859.

Some have claimed to find support for the Bacon theory in the word "honorificabilitudinitatibus" from *Love's Labour's Lost* (V,1,41). "Honorificabilitudinitatibus", they claim, is an anagram of

hi ludi F. Baconis nati tuiti orbi

which is Latin, and means

These plays F. Bacon's offspring preserved for the world.

The only intelligent thing to be said about this is: the longer the word, the more likely you are to be able to make a sentence out of it.

12 Delia Bacon was no relation to Sir Francis Bacon, although in later years she claimed she was.

---

13 **anagram:** Anagramm (Umstellung von Buchstaben zu anderen Wörtern mit neuem Sinn).

Searching for Cyphers
by David Crystal and Ben Crystal

In *The Great Cryptogram* (1888), Ignatius Donnelly devoted two large volumes to [...] *Francis Bacon's Cipher in the So-called Shakespeare Plays*. Devising a complex system of recurring numbers, roots and arithmetical operations, he demonstrated to his own satisfaction (but to few others at the time or since) the existence of hidden messages in his facsimile of the First Folio which gave clues to the 'real' author.

Here are two examples which illustrate the way Donnelly's method works:

> On p. 53 of the Histories he finds the line "I have a gammon of Bacon and two razes of ginger". He calculates that *Bacon* is the 371st word on the page, divides this by the page number and gets 7. This then becomes the cypher number for Bacon.
> On p. 67, *St Albans*[13] is the 402nd word on the page. Divide 402 by 67 and you get 6, which is the corresponding number for St Albans.

He then applied this method to many thousands of words, and was able to find such messages hidden within the text as:

13 Francis Bacon was Viscount St Albans.

5 **to devise s.th.:** etwas erdenken, erfinden, sich etwas ausdenken. |
5f. **recurring:** periodisch. | 13f. **gammon:** hier: Keule. | 14 **raze:** (Ingwer-)Wurzel.

Francis Bacon Nicholas Bacon's Son.

He works out a single root-number, 327, to obtain the message:

More low [Marlowe] or Shak'st spur never writ a word of them.

It was an amazing feat of misdirected energy, but it involved hundreds of arbitrary and inconsistent decisions (such as whether a hyphenated word would count as one word or two). Nor is it difficult to turn such a method against its author – and indeed, in the same year, someone used Donnelly's exact procedure to show the following message hidden within the plays:

Master Will i a Jack Spur writ this play and was engaged at the Curtain.

Shakespeare, it seems, was the author after all.

Authorship of the Plays
by Richard Armour

Whoever wrote Shakespeare's plays, one thing is certain. It could not possibly have been Shakespeare. That would have been too obvious. Besides, the man had so little edu-

---

2 **to obtain:** bekommen, erhalten. | 6 **feat:** (beachtliche) Leistung. | 7 **arbitrary:** willkürlich. | **inconsistent:** widersprüchlich. | 8 **hyphenated:** mit Bindestrich geschrieben. | 11 **procedure:** Vorgehensweise. | 20 **obvious:** offensichtlich.

WILLIAM SHAKESPEARE, HIS METHOD OF WORK

cation that he could hardly read a play, much less write one. It is true that he might have attended school during the Lost Years, but if, as some believe, he was a schoolteacher at that time, he would have been far too busy teaching to learn anything. At any rate, it is a contemptible attack on higher education (an early instance of anti-intellectualism) to suggest that a person who never went to college could have written poetry that is too difficult for most college students.

Moreover, as anyone knows who has viewed the various Shakespeare signatures[14], if he had written the plays they would have been illegible. [...] Actors, given their parts in Shakespeare's handwriting, would have groped their way across the stage, overcome by emotion and eyestrain. Publication would have been impossible, unless the compositor was sufficiently creative to substitute poetry of his own for some undecipherable passage.

Obviously we must turn elsewhere for the authorship of Shakespeare's plays.

One person who may have written them is Francis Bacon, who had to be doing *something* when he wasn't serving as a Member of Parliament, acting as Solicitor-General, Attorney-General, and Lord Keeper,* and writing Bacon's

---

14 See p. 11 f.
* Keeping lords was a full-time job in itself.

2f. **Lost Years:** Die Jahre 1585–92. | 5 **contemptible:** verachtenswert. | 13 **to grope one's way:** sich tasten. | 14 **eyestrain:** Überanstrengung der Augen. | 15f. **compositor:** Setzer. | 17 **undecipherable:** unentzifferbar. | **passage:** (Text-)Passage. | 22f. **Solicitor-General / Attorney-General / Lord Keeper:** Generalstaatsanwalt, Generalfiskal, Großsiegelbewahrer (hohe Ämter, die Bacon 1607, 1613 bzw. 1617 bekleidete).

The Authorship Question 55

Complete Works. If his own dull prose treatises and didactic essays are utterly unlike the imaginative poetry and inspired characterizations he wrote under the name of Shakespeare, it is indisputable proof that Bacon suffered not only from heartburn and Raleigh's Disease* but schizophrenia. Why Bacon chose the pen name** of Shakespeare for his dramatic works is probably explained by his fear of what ham actors would do to plays under his own name. Also, he had said in one of his essays that "some books are to be chewed and digested." The librarians were after him, and he needed an alias.

Another person who may have written Shapespeare's plays is the Earl of Oxford. This gentleman had one advantage over Shakespeare when it came to writing plays: he had a title. Plots were everywhere,*** but titles were hard to come by. Having lent his name to the University of Ox-

---

 * Brought on by antagonizing Queen Elizabeth.
 ** He was in the pen at the time, serving a term for bribery.
*** See the Gunpowder Plot, etc.

---

1 **treatise:** Abhandlung. | 2 **utterly:** vollkommen. | 4 **indisputable:** unbestreitbar. | 5 **heartburn:** Sodbrennen. | 6 **pen name:** Pseudonym. | 8 **ham actor:** Schmierenkomödiant. | 10 **to chew s.th.:** etwas kauen; (fig.) etwas durchdenken. | **to digest s.th.:** etwas verdauen; (fig.) etwas durchdenken, verarbeiten. | **librarian:** Bibliothekar. | 11 **alias:** Deckname. | 15 **title:** 1. (Adels-)Titel; 2. Eigentumsrecht. | **plot:** 1. Parzelle, Bauland; 2. Plot, Handlung (in einem literarischen Werk). | 16 **to lend one's name to s.th.:** seinen Namen für etwas hergeben. | 17 **to antagonize s.o.:** sich jdm. widersetzen. Der englische Seefahrer, Entdecker und Schriftsteller Sir Walter Raleigh (1552 oder 1554–1618) heiratete heimlich eine der Hofdamen Elisabeths I., fiel dadurch in Ungnade bei der Königin und wurde vom Hof verstoßen.

ford, the Oxford Dictionary, the Oxford Movement, and a type of low brogan, the Earl thought it only fair to borrow someone else's name when he became a dramatist. Why he chose the name of Shakespeare is not known. Perhaps he closed his eyes and pointed at a name in the telephone book. Then again he may have liked the sound of the Oxford Edition of Shakespeare but felt that the Oxford Edition of Oxford would be overdoing it.

However, the most likely author of Shakespeare's plays is Christopher Marlowe, who, having attended the University of Cambridge, had taken a course in Elizabethan Drama and knew all about tragic flaws, comic relief, etc. One thing that made it difficult for Marlowe to write Shakespeare's plays was the fact that he was killed in a tavern brawl before most of the plays were written.* Some maintain that Marlowe was not killed but only fatally wounded, lingering on for twenty years and writing as if each day were his last. Others believe that the later plays were written by Marlowe's descendants, often referred to as "Marlowe's mighty line." Still others contend that Marlowe wrote the plays in his tomb, where he could work uninterruptedly and be in close contact with the nether world. These researchers, who keep their ears to the ground and

---

* And probably before paying his bill. See the Case of the Red Lion Inn vs. the Estate of Christopher Marlowe.

---

2 **brogan:** *brogue:* Herrenschuh. | 8 **to overdo s.th.:** etwas übertreiben, bei etwas zu weit gehen. | 12 **tragic flaw:** Charakterschwäche, tragischer Fehler. | **comic relief:** befreiende Komik. | 15 **brawl:** Schlägerei. | 15 f. **to maintain:** behaupten. | 17 **to linger:** dahinsiechen. | 20 **to contend that ...:** behaupten, geltend machen, dass ... | 21 **tomb:** Grab, Gruft. | 22 **the nether world:** die Unterwelt.

go into a frenzy whenever they think they hear the faint scratching of a quill, have been opening tombs and prying off coffin lids for years. The most recent tomb in which Marlowe was not discovered was that of his friend and protector, Sir Thomas Walsingham. But for the threatening inscription over the grave of William Shakespeare, Gent., of Stratford, they would long since have had the stones up, prepared to exclaim triumphantly to the figure rising from his writing desk, "Mr. Marlowe, I presume."

The time has not yet come to speak of the Age of Oxford or the Baconian Theater, or to revise Shakespeare courses in college catalogues to read: "English 38a,b. Marlowe. Year course, 10 MWF. ... English 142b. Advanced Marlowe. Second semester. 11 TThS." But one never knows.*

If, by chance, Shakespeare's works were not written by Bacon, the Earl of Oxford, or Marlowe, who could the author have been? Passing over the ingenious but inadequately documented cases recently made for the Piltdown Man,

---

* Does one?

---

1 **frenzy**: Rasen, Raserei. | 2 **to pry s.th. off**: etwas (Deckel o. Ä.) aufstemmen, gewaltsam öffnen. | 4f. **protector**: Beschützer. | 5 **but for ...**: wäre nicht ... gewesen. | 9 **Mr. Marlowe, I presume**: Anspielung auf den Engländer Sir Henry Morton Stanley (d.i. John Rowlands, 1841–1904), der 1871 dem in Zentralafrika verschollenen Entdecker und Missionar David Livingstone in Ujiji mit den Worten »Dr Livingstone, I presume« begegnete. | 13 **MWF**: Abk. für *Monday, Wednesday, Friday*. | 14 **TThS**: Abk. für *Tuesday, Thursday, Saturday*. | 17 **ingenious**: raffiniert, genial. | 18 **Piltdown Man**: 1912 legte Charles Dawson (1864–1916) Schädel und Unterkiefer einer bis dahin unbekannten Menschenart vor (*Eoanthropus dawsoni*). Erst 1953 gelang der Nachweis, dass die Fragmente, angeblich aus Piltdown, East Sussex, einem Orang-Utan bzw. einem modernen Menschen entstammten.

Whistler's Father, and Noel Coward, and brushing aside (with a large brush we keep for this purpose) the suggestion that it was Queen Elizabeth (who was really a man) or the Earl of Essex (who was really a woman), we come to a conclusion.

A Legendary Blues Guitarist
by Ben Crystal

It doesn't matter who Shakespeare might have been, because who he was isn't as important to us as *when* he was and *what* he did. But so little about the man has been discovered, his life has become a bit of an enigma. And this seems to make people doubt that he wrote the plays.

This is not a rare thing. Almost nothing is known about the legendary blues guitarist and singer Robert Johnson (1911–38). Many consider him to be the king of the Delta blues singers, yet there are only two photos of him in existence, almost nothing is known about his early life, there are varying stories surrounding his death (the most popular being that his whisky was poisoned by a jealous juke joint

---

1 **Whistler's Father:** Anspielung auf das unter dem Namen »Whistler's Mother« weltbekannte Ölgemälde des Amerikaners James Abbot McNeill Whistler (1834–1903) »Arrangement in Grey and Black No. 1«. | **Coward:** Noel C. (1899–1973), englischer Schauspieler, Schriftsteller und Komponist. | **to brush s.th. aside:** etwas abtun, ignorieren. | 11 **enigma:** Rätsel. | 15 f. **Delta blues:** Richtung des Blues, die in den 1910er Jahren im Mississippi-Delta entstand. | 18 **varying:** unterschiedlich, voneinander abweichend. | **surrounding his death:** um seinen Tod. | 19 **juke joint:** Lokal (*joint*), in dem Musikautomaten zur Verfügung stehen.

owner, who'd caught Johnson flirting with his wife), and there are three different ideas about where he's buried. All we really have to go on are the 29 songs and a handful of alternative takes that he recorded. But he was so good, a legend has developed around him that he wasn't able to play the guitar until he went to a crossroads at midnight and the devil tuned his guitar for him. Not happy with the idea that he could naturally be that talented, people developed a magical reason for his talent. Just like Shakespeare.

---

4 **take:** Take, (Musik-)Aufnahme. | 6 **crossroads** (pl.): Kreuzung. | 7 **to tune:** (Musikinstrument) stimmen.

The Works

William Shakespeare's *Star Wars*
  by Ian Doescher

Dramatis Personae

CHORUS

LUKE SKYWALKER, *a boy of Tatooine*
OWEN LARS, *his uncle*
BERU LARS, *his aunt*
OBI-WAN KENOBI, *a Jedi knight*
PRINCESS LEIA ORGANA, *of Alderaan*
HAN SOLO, *a smuggler*
CHEWBACCA, *a Wookie and Han's first mate*
DARTH VADER, *a Sith Lord*
GOVERNOR TARKIN, *of the Imperial army*
C-3PO, *a droid*
R2-D2, *his companion*
JABBA THE HUTT, *a boss*
GREEDO, *his bounty hunter*
WEDGE ANTILLES, *a rebel pilot*
BIGGS DARKLIGHTER, *a rebel pilot*

REBEL LEADERS, CHIEF PILOTS, STORMTROOPERS,
CAPTAINS, COMMANDERS, ADMIRALS, GUARDS,
JAWAS, DROIDS, TUSKEN RAIDERS, BAR PATRONS,
IMPERIAL LEADERS, *and* REBEL PILOTS

Prologue

Outer space.
Enter Chorus.

CHORUS. It is a period of civil war.
  The spaceships of the rebels, striking swift
  From base unseen, have gain'd a vict'ry o'er
  The cruel Galactic Empire, now adrift.
  Amidst the battle, rebel spies prevail'd
  And stole the plans to a space station vast,
  Whose pow'rful beams will later be unveil'd
  And crush a planet: 'tis the DEATH STAR blast.
  Pursu'd by agents sinister and cold,
  Now Princess Leia to her home doth flee,
  Deliv'ring plans and a new hope they hold:
  Of bringing freedom to the galaxy.
  In time so long ago begins our play,
  In star-crossed galaxy far, far away.
Exit.

---

1 **prologue:** Prolog, Vorspiel. | 6 **base:** Stützpunkt. | 7 **adrift:** treibend. | 8 **to prevail:** sich durchsetzen, siegen. | 11 **to crush:** vernichten. | **blast:** hier: zerstörerischer Strahl. | 12 **to pursue s.o.:** jdn. verfolgen. | **sinister:** unheimlich. | 17 **star-crossed:** unheilvoll; Anspielung auf die unglücklich Liebenden Romeo und Julia (*Romeo and Juliet*, Prologue, 6).

Scene 1

Aboard the rebel ship.
Enter C-3PO and R2-D2.

C-3PO. Now is the summer of our happiness
    Made winter by this sudden, fierce attack!
    Our ship is under siege, I know not how.
    O hast thou heard? The main reactor fails!
    We shall most surely be destroy'd by this.
    I'll warrant madness lies herein!
R2-D2.   – Beep beep,
    Beep, beep, meep, squeak, beep, beep, beep, whee!
C-3PO. – We're doomed.
    The princess shall have no escape this time!
    I fear this battle doth portend the end
    Of the Rebellion. O! What misery!
    Exeunt C-3PO and R2-D2.
CHORUS. Now watch, amaz'd, as swiftly through the door
    The army of the Empire flyeth in.
    And as the troopers through the passage pour,
    They murder sev'ral dozen rebel men.
    Fighting begins.

---

9 **to warrant** (arch.): glauben, sicher sein. | 14 **to portend s.th.**: etwas ankündigen, auf etwas hindeuten.

King Lear

The Fool Disappears | Gloucester is Blinded *then Dies of Shock* | Cornwall is Stabbed | Oswald is Stabbed | Goneril Stabs Herself *and* Poisons her sister, Regan | Edmund is Stabbed | Cordelia is Hanged | and Lear dies of Grief

Titus Andronicus

Alarbus's Arms and Legs are Cut Off, *then* he is Thrown into a Fire | Chiron and Demetrius are Stabbed *then* Baked into a Pie which Titus feeds to Tamora | Tamora dies of Indigestion | Lavinia's Hands and Tongue are Cut Off *then* she is Stabbed | The Nurse is Stabbed

Mutius is Stabbed | Bassanius is Stabbed | Martius and Quintus are Beheaded | The Clown is Hanged | Saturninus is Stabbed | Titus is Stabbed | and Aaron is Buried to his Neck *and* Starves

Coriolanus and Timon of Athens   Bonus: The Winter's Tale

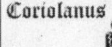 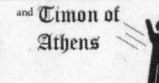 

Coriolanus is Cut to Pieces | Just throws Himself Away. | Antigonus Exits, Pursued by a Bear

The Skinhead Hamlet
Shakespeare's play translated into modern English
by Richard Curtis

"Our hope was to achieve something like the effect
of the New English Bible" – Eds

Act 1

Scene 1

The Battlements of Elsinore Castle.
Enter Hamlet, followed by Ghost.

GHOST. Oi! Mush!
HAMLET. Yer?
GHOST. I was fucked!
   Exit Ghost.
HAMLET. O fuck.
   Exit Hamlet.

---

5 **New English Bible:** ironische Anspielung auf die 1948 begonnene Neuübersetzung der originären biblischen Texte ins Englische (Neubearbeitung 1989: *Revised English Bible*), bei der man Wert auf ein natürliches Englisch legte. | **Eds:** Abk. für *Editors* (pl.): Herausgeber. | 8 **battlements:** Zinnen. | 10 **Oi! Mush!:** Grußformel (*mush:* Kerl).

Scene 2

The Throne Room.
Enter King Claudius, Gertrude, Hamlet and Court.

CLAUDIUS. Oi! You, Hamlet, give over!
HAMLET. Fuck off, won't you?
   Exit Claudius, Gertrude, Court.
HAMLET (*alone*). They could have fucking waited.
   Enter Horatio.
HORATIO. Oi! Whatcha cock!
HAMLET. Weeeeey!
   Exeunt.

Scene 3

Ophelia's Bedroom.
Enter Ophelia and Laertes.

LAERTES. I'm fucking off now. Watch Hamlet doesn't slip you one while I'm gone.
OPHELIA. I'll be fucked if he does.
   Exeunt.

---

2 **Throne Room:** Thronsaal. | 4 **give over!:** hör doch auf! | 9 **Whatcha cock:** Grußformel; wohl aus *what cheer, cock?* (*cock:* Kerl). | 15 f. **to slip s.o. one:** mit jdm. schlafen (*to slip:* rutschen; stecken).

Scene 4

The Battlements.
Enter Horatio, Hamlet and Ghost.

GHOST. Oi! Mush, get on with it!
HAMLET. Who did it then?
GHOST. That wanker Claudius. He poured fucking poison in my fucking ear!
HAMLET. Fuck me!
Exeunt.

Act 2

Scene 1

A Corridor in the Castle.
Enter Hamlet reading. Enter Polonius.

POLONIUS. Oi! You!
HAMLET. Fuck off, grandad!
Exit Polonius. Enter Rosencrantz and Guildenstern.
ROSENCRANTZ and GUILDENSTERN. Oi! Oi! Mucca!
HAMLET. Fuck off, the pair of you!
Exit Rosencrantz and Guildenstern.
HAMLET (*alone*). To fuck or be fucked.
Enter Ophelia.
OPHELIA. My Lord!

---

6 **wanker:** Wichser. | 17 **mucca** (coll.): Kumpel, Bruder.

The Works   69

HAMLET. Fuck off to a nunnery!
   They exit in different directions.

Act 3

Scene 1

Throne Room.
Enter Players and all Court.

1 PLAYER. Full thirty time hath Phoebus cart …
CLAUDIUS. I'll be fucked if I watch any more of this crap.
   Exeunt.

Scene 2

Gertrude's Bedchamber.
Enter Hamlet, to Gertrude.

HAMLET. Oi! Slag!
GERTRUDE. Watch your fucking mouth, kid!
POLONIUS (*from behind the curtain*). Too right.
HAMLET. Who the fuck was that?
   He stabs Polonius through the arras.
POLONIUS. Fuck!

---

1 **nunnery:** (Nonnen-)Kloster. | 8 **crap:** Müll, Mist. | 13 **slag:** Schlampe. | 15 **too right:** nur zu wahr!, stimmt genau! | 17 **to stab:** ab-, erstechen. | **arras:** (gewirkter) Wandbehang.

HAMLET. Fuck! I thought it was that other wanker.
Exeunt.

Act 4

Scene 1

Court Room.

CLAUDIUS. Fuck off to England then!
HAMLET. Delighted, mush.

Scene 2

Throne Room.
Ophelia, Gertrude and Claudius.

OPHELIA. Here, cop a whack of this.
She hands Gertrude some rosemary and exits.
CLAUDIUS. She's fucking round the twist, isn't she?
GERTRUDE (*looking out the window*).
    There is a willow grows aslant the brook.
CLAUDIUS. Get on with it, slag.

---

11 **cop a whack:** etwa: probier mal das hier. | 12 **rosemary:** Rosmarin. In *Hamlet* IV,5 verteilt die wahnsinnig gewordene Ophelia Blumen und Kräuter an die Anwesenden. | 13 **round the twist:** durchgedreht. | 15 **There is a willow grows aslant the brook:** So beschreibt Königin Gertrude in *Hamlet* IV,7,165 den Ort, wo Ophelia ertrunken ist (*willow*: Weidenbaum; *aslant*: quer über; *brook*: Bach).

GERTRUDE. Ophelia's gone and fucking drowned!
CLAUDIUS. Fuck! Laertes isn't half going to be browned off.
Exeunt.

Scene 3

A Corridor.

LAERTES (*alone*). I'm going to fucking do this lot.
  Enter Claudius.
CLAUDIUS. I didn't fucking do it, mate. It was that wanker Hamlet.
LAERTES. Well, fuck him.

Act 5

Scene 1

Hamlet's Bedchamber.
Hamlet and Horatio seated.

HAMLET. I got this feeling I'm going to cop it, Horatio, and, you know, I couldn't give a flying fuck.
  Exeunt.

2f. **browned off:** verärgert. | 7 **to do:** hier: erledigen. | 9 **mate:** Kumpel. | 16 **I'm going to cop it:** mich wird's erwischen.

72 The Works

Scene 2

Large Hall.
Enter Hamlet, Laertes, Court, Gertrude, Claudius.

LAERTES. Oi, wanker: let's get on with it!
HAMLET. Delighted, fuckface.
They fight and both are poisoned by the poisoned sword.
LAERTES. Fuck!
HAMLET. Fuck!
The Queen drinks.
GERTRUDE. Fucking odd wine!
CLAUDIUS. You drunk the wrong fucking cup, you stupid cow!
HAMLET (*pouring the poison down Claudius' throat*). Well, fuck you!
CLAUDIUS. I'm fair and squarely fucked.
LAERTES. Oi, mush: no hard feelings, he?
HAMLET. Yer.
Laertes dies.
HAMLET. Oi! Horatio!
HORATIO. Yer?
HAMLET. I'm fucked. The rest is fucking silence.
Hamlet dies.
HORATIO. Fuck: that was no ordinary wanker, you know.
Enter Fortinbras.
FORTINBRAS. What the fuck's going on here?
HORATIO. A fucking mess, that's for sure.

---

11 **odd:** merkwürdig. | 16 **fair and square(ly):** ganz klar, genau.

The Works 73

FORTINBRAS. No kidding. I see Hamlet's fucked.
HORATIO. Yer.
FORTINBRAS. Fucking shame: fucking good bloke.
HORATIO. Too fucking right.
FORTINBRAS. Fuck this for a lark then. Let's piss off.
Exeunt with alarums.

The Famed "To Be or Not To Be" Scene from *Hamlet*
  by WILLIAM SHAKESPEARE
  A modern verse rendition
  by Desmond Olivier Dingle

Act 1

Scene: A street in Denmark. Enter Hamlet.

HAMLET. To be or not to be.
    That is the problem as I see it at this juncture, basically.
    Whether it is nobler in the mind to suffer
    All the set-backs and what-not that occur, generally
                                    speaking,
    Through life.
    Put up with the whole bleeding treadmill, in other
                                       words, or simply

---

1 **no kidding:** was du nicht sagst. | 5 **Fuck this for a lark:** Ich hab die Schnauze voll. | 6 **alarum** (arch.): *alarm*. | 9 **verse rendition:** Versversion. | 10 **Desmond Olivier Dingle:** Pseudonym des englischen Schauspielers und Schriftstellers Patrick Barlow (geb. 1947). | 14 **at this juncture:** zum jetzigen Zeitpunkt. | 16 **set-back:** Rückschlag. | **what-not:** was sonst noch alles. | 19 **bleeding:** verdammt. | **treadmill:** Tretmühle.

John Philip Kemble (1757–1823) as Hamlet.
Painting (1801) by Sir Thomas Lawrence

> Jack it in.
> To die, to sleep – no more,
> That's what's on my mind, basically.
> I could say if I done this, obviously,
> I'd have no more concerns, no more personal
> problems or
> Financial constraints.
> But,
> On the other hand,
> I'd be dead.
> Which is a bit of a problem
> When you think about it.
> *Exeunt.*

A Soliloquy Simplified: "To Be, or the Contrary?"
by Sir Arthur Quiller-Couch

To be, or the contrary? Whether the former or the latter be preferable would seem to admit of some difference of opinion; the answer in the present case being of an affirmative or of a negative character according as to whether one elects on the one hand to mentally suffer the disfavour of fortune, albeit in an extreme degree, or on the other to boldly envisage adverse conditions in the prospect of bringing them to a conclusion. The condition of sleep is similar to,

---

1 **to jack it in:** aufgeben. | 7 **constraints:** Beschränkungen. | 13 **exeunt:** richtig: *exit*. | 14 **soliloquy** [sə'lɪləkwi]: Monolog. | 17 **to admit of s.th.** (poet.): etwas zulassen. | 18 **affirmative:** positiv, zustimmend. | 21 **albeit:** obgleich. | 22 **to envisage** [ɪn'vɪzɪdʒ] (poet.): einer Sache (Gefahr) ins Gesicht schauen. | **adverse:** ungünstig, widrig.

if not indistinguishable from, that of death; and with the addition of finality the former might be considered identical with the latter: so that in this connection it might be argued with regard to sleep that, could the addition be effected, a termination would be put to the endurance of a multiplicity of inconveniences, not to mention a number of downright evils incidental to our fallen humanity, and thus a consummation achieved of a most gratifying nature.

The Tragedy of *Othello*
by WILLIAM SHAKESPEARE
A modern verse rendition
by Desmond Olivier Dingle

Act 1

Scene: A street in Vienna.
Enter Othello and Desdemona.

DESDEMONA. Welcome, noble Moor!
OTHELLO. Ah! My lovely wife Desdemona!
DESDEMONA. Good trip?

---

1 **indistinguishable:** ununterscheidbar. | 2 **finality:** Endgültigkeit. | 5 **termination:** Beendigung. | **endurance:** Ausdauer, Durchhaltevermögen. | 6 **multiplicity:** Vielzahl. | **inconvenience:** Unannehmlichkeit. | 7 **downright:** völlig, absolut. | **(to be) incidental to s.th:** mit etwas einhergehen. | 8 **consummation:** Erfüllung. | **gratifying:** befriedigend. | 15 **Vienna:** absichtliche Verwechslung der Handlungsschauplätze; in *Othello* sind Venedig (*Venice*) und Zypern (*Cyprus*) Orte der Handlung.

OTHELLO. Yes, thank you very much.
Enter Iago.
IAGO. Hello from me too, by the way.
OTHELLO. Hello Iago. This is my wife Desdemona, by the way.
IAGO. Hello Desdemona.
DESDEMONA. Hello, Iago.
IAGO. Anyway, don't mind me.
OTHELLO. Sorry?
IAGO. I just need to check a couple of things.
OTHELLO. Fair enough.
Iago checks a number of maps, pens and papers etc. in the bureau.
OTHELLO. Anyway, I hope you have been true to me!
DESDEMONA. I beg your pardon?
OTHELLO. While I've been away in various wars in Cyprus?
DESDEMONA. Of course I have, my noble Moor.
OTHELLO. Because if you haven't, I may be driven mad!
DESDEMONA. Good heavens! I didn't realise that about your personality!
IAGO (*aside*). Nor did I!
OTHELLO. *And* strangle you on your bed!
DESDEMONA. Good Lord!
OTHELLO. So no hanky-panky!
DESDEMONA. Pardon?
OTHELLO. With a handkerchief, for instance!

---

13 **bureau:** Sekretär, Schreibtisch. | 14 **to be true to s.o.:** jdm. treu sein. | 23 **to strangle s.o.:** jdn. erwürgen. | 25 **hanky-panky:** Techtelmechtel.

DESDEMONA. Hanky-panky with a handkerchief?
OTHELLO. Hanky-panky with a hanky!
DESDEMONA. Keep your hair on!
IAGO (*aside*). Good heavens!
An awkward moment.
OTHELLO. I'm sorry!
DESDEMONA. Blimey!
OTHELLO. I'm a little overwrought.
DESDEMONA. I'll say!
Another awkward moment. Iago continues checking the bureau.
IAGO. Anyway …
OTHELLO. I humbly do beseech you of your pardon
  For too much loving you.
DESDEMONA. Right.
Another awkward moment. They look at one another.
OTHELLO. So have you got it?
DESDEMONA. What?
OTHELLO. The hanky!
DESDEMONA. The hanky?
OTHELLO. You haven't got it?
DESDEMONA. *NO!!*
OTHELLO. So who has got it?
DESDEMONA. I DON'T KNOW WHO'S GOT IT!!
OTHELLO. Right, that's it!

---

2 **hanky:** Kurzform von *handkerchief*: Stofftaschentuch. | 3 **Keep your hair on!:** Immer mit der Ruhe! | 7 **blimey:** du meine Güte! | 8 **overwrought:** überreizt, mit den Nerven am Ende. | 13 **to beseech s.o. of s.th.** (arch., poet.) jdn. um etwas bitten. | 15 **right:** in Ordnung.

DESDEMONA. What?
Othello strangles Desdemona.
DESDEMONA. Agggh!
Iago is still checking the bureau.
IAGO. Don't mind me.
OTHELLO. What have I done?

INTERVAL

Act 5

A few seconds later.
Enter Brabantio, The Doge of Venice and Giorgio Armani.

GIORGIO ARMANI. What has happened?
OTHELLO. It is the very error of the moon.
   She comes more near the earth than she was wont
   And makes men mad.
ALL. A likely story!
They murder Othello.
OTHELLO. Agggggh!
Exeunt Brabantio, The Doge of Venice and Giorgio Armani.
There is an awkward silence.

---

10 **Brabantio:** Desdemonas Vater. | 12 ff. **It is the very error ... makes men mad:** *Othello* V,2,118–120. Der Irrtum des Mondes besteht darin, dass er näher an die Erde als gewöhnlich kommt und die Menschen in den Wahnsinn treibt (*she:* der Mond ist im Englischen Femininum). | 18 **exeunt:** richtig: *exit*.

IAGO. So ... er ...
Re-enter Brabantio, The Doge of Venice and Giorgio Armani.
GIORGIO ARMANI. What?
IAGO. Thanks to all at once and to each one,
   Whom we invite to see us crowned at Scone.
   A slight pause.
ALL. Marvellous.
Exeunt Brabantio, The Doge of Venice and Giorgio Armani.
Exeunt Iago, having closed the bureau.

FINIS

Shakespeare According to Gyles Brandreth

Just as the famous Dr. Bowdler sought to improve the works of Shakespeare by cutting out or altering all indelicacies (turning "bed" into "bridal chariot," for example), I seek to improve his plays by dropping a different letter from each one. I began with *Hamlet*, from which I scrupulously excluded the letter *i*. Here's how the most famous of all soliloquies turned out:

6 **Whom we invite to see us crowned at Scone:** letzte Zeile aus *Macbeth* (V,11,41). Mit diesen Worten lädt Malcolm die Anwesenden zu seiner Krönung in Scone. | 13 **Brandreth:** Gyles B. (geb. 1948), englischer Schriftsteller und ehemaliger konservativer Abgeordneter. | 15f. **indelicacies:** etwa: unfeine Ausdrücke. | 16 **bridal chariot:** etwa: Hochzeitswagen (*chariot* [poet.]: [Streit-]Wagen). | 17 **to drop** (fig.): weglassen, streichen. | 18f. **scrupulously:** gründlich, peinlich sauber. | 20 **soliloquy** [səˈlɪləkwi]: Monolog.

> To be, or not to be; that's the query:
> Whether you would be nobler to suffer mentally
> The stones and arrows of outrageous fortune,
> Or to take arms to oppose a sea of troubles,
> And through combat end them? To pass on, to sleep;
> No more …

And so it goes on for five whole acts until Hamlet expires uttering the deathless line:

> The rest be hush-hush.

From *Macbeth* I dropped *a* and *e*. Here is the hero (McB'th) having one of his hallucinations:

> Is it thy tiny sword in front I'm glimpsing,
> With its blunt bit pointing to my wrist? I wish to
>   touch it:
> I find I'm no good doing it, but I spy it still …

From the whole of *Twelfth Night* I excluded *l*, the twelfth letter from the beginning of the alphabet, and *o*, the twelfth letter from the end of the alphabet. In my version of the play, Orsino launches the proceedings with these lyrical lines:

---

7 **to expire:** verscheiden. | 8 **to utter s.th.:** etwas von sich geben. | **deathless:** unsterblich. | 9 **hush-hush:** Schweigen, streng geheim. | 12 **to glimpse:** flüchtig sehen. | 16 **to exclude s.th.:** etwas ausschließen. | 19 **launch proceedings:** die Geschehnisse, das Geschehen in Gang bringen.

> If music be desire's sustenance, make music yet;
> Give me excessive music, that, surfeiting,
> The appetite may sicken, and thus die …

Currently I'm working on *Othello* without the *o*'s. It isn't easy, but what is art without suffering?

The Curse of *Mac*…

It is said to bring bad luck to mention the title of the Shakespearean play that takes place mainly in Scotland. Actors and theatre managers call it "The Scottish Play" instead. If you mention the name of the play by mistake, there are several things you can do to set things right again and bring yourself out of danger:

- Leave the room, close the door behind you. Turn around three times, swear, knock on the door, and ask to be let back in.
- Walk around the theatre three times.
- Quote Hamlet: "Angels and ministers of grace defend us!" (I,4,20)

It is also said to bring bad luck to quote from "The Scottish Play" if you are not inside a theatre. If you quote some lines from "The Scottish Play" while not inside a theatre, then you should quote the same number of lines from one of Shakespeare's comedies (*A Midsummer Night's Dream* is probably the best choice) to put things right again.

---

1 **sustenance:** Nahrung. | 2 **to surfeit** ['sɜːfɪt] **o.s.:** sich überessen. | 11 **to set things right:** alles wieder in Ordnung bringen.

You don't believe in superstition and curses? Here are some nasty things that have happened during rehearsals and performances of the Shakespearean play that takes place mainly in Scotland.

- During the play's first performance, Hal Berridge, the boy playing Lady Macbeth, died backstage, and (tradition says) Shakespeare had to play the part.
- In a production in Amsterdam, in 1672, the actor playing Macbeth used a real dagger, and killed the actor playing Duncan in front of the audience.
- During rival performances of the play in New York, in 1849, a riot broke out and over twenty people died.
- In John Gielgud's 1942 production, three actors died – Duncan and two of the witches – and the set designer committed suicide.
- Two fires and seven robberies happened during David Leary's 1971 production.
- Cambridge Shakespeare Company, 2001: Macduff injured his back, Lady Macbeth hit her head, Ross broke his toe and two cedar trees crashed to the ground, destroying the set.[15]

15 This list is drawn from David Crystal and Ben Crystal, "Superstitious?", in: D. C. and B. C., *The Shakespeare Miscellany*, London: Penguin, 2005, p. 177.

1 **superstition:** Aberglaube. | 2 **rehearsal:** (Theater-)Probe. | 12 **riot:** Krawall, Ausschreitungen. | 13 **Gielgud:** Sir John G. (1904–2000), berühmter englischer Schauspieler. Seine Darstellung des Hamlet, den er zum ersten Mal 1929 spielte, galt lange als maßgeblich. | 14 **set designer:** Bühnenbildner. | 20 **cedar:** Zeder.

Not everybody believes in the curse, however. Here is what the British director Gregory Doran said on the first day of rehearsals for a production of *Macbeth* in 1999:

> We're calling it *Macbeth* ... Not *Mackers*, not *The Scottish Play*, none of the euphemisms. *Macbeth*, *Macbeth*, *Macbeth* – there, I've said it and haven't been struck down. There's supposed to be a curse on this play. Bollocks! The only curse is that it's so hard to do.[16]

The Macbeth Murder Mystery
by James Thurber

"It was a stupid mistake to make," said the American woman I had met at my hotel in the English lake country, "but it was on the counter with the other Penguin books – the little sixpenny ones, you know, with the paper covers – and I supposed of course it was a detective story. All the others were detective stories. I'd read all the others, so I bought this one without really looking at it carefully. You can imagine how mad I was when I found it was Shakespeare." I murmured something sympathetically. "I don't see why the Penguin-books people had to get out Shakespeare's plays in the same size and everything as the detective stories," went on my companion. "I think they have different-colored jackets," I said. "Well, I didn't notice that," she said. "Anyway, I got real comfy in bed that night and all ready to

---

16 Ibid., p. 178.

5 **euphemism** ['juːfəmɪzᵊm]: Euphemismus, Beschönigung. | 7 **bollocks:** Quatsch. | 19 **to murmur:** murmeln. | 24 **comfy:** bequem, gemütlich.

read a good mystery story and here I had 'The Tragedy of
Macbeth' – a book for high-school students. Like 'Ivanhoe.'" "Or 'Lorna Doone,'" I said. "Exactly," said the American lady. "And I was just crazy for a good Agatha Christie,
or something. Hercule Poirot is my favorite detective." "Is
he the rabbity one?" I asked. "Oh, no," said my crime-
fiction expert. "He's the Belgian one. You're thinking of
Mr. Pinkerton, the one that helps Inspector Bull. He's good,
too."

Over her second cup of tea my companion began to tell
the plot of a detective story that had fooled her completely – it seems it was the old family doctor all the time. But I
cut in on her. "Tell me," I said. "Did you read 'Macbeth'?" "I
had to read it," she said. "There wasn't a scrap of anything
else to read in the whole room." "Did you like it?" I asked.
"No, I did not," she said decisively. "In the first place, I
don't think for a moment that Macbeth did it." I looked at
her blankly. "Did what?" I asked. "I don't think for a mo-

2f. **"Ivanhoe":** Roman (1820) des schottischen Schriftstellers Sir Walter
Scott (1771–1832) und Name der Hauptfigur Sir Wilfred of Ivanhoe. |
3 **"Lorna Doone":** Roman (1869) des englischen Schriftstellers Richard
Doddridge Blackmore (1825–1900). | 4 **to be crazy for s.th.:** verrückt
nach etwas sein. | **Christie:** Agatha Ch. (1890–1976), englische Schrift-
stellerin; verfasste über 70 Kriminalromane, darunter *Murder on the
Orient Express* (1934) und *Death on the Nile* (1937). Der belgische Detektiv
Hercule Poirot ist neben Miss Marple ihre berühmteste Schöpfung. |
8 **Mr. Pinkerton:** Der Waliser Evan Pinkerton und dessen Freund Inspector Bull von Scotland Yard sind Schöpfungen der amerikanischen
Schriftstellerin Zenith Jones Brown (1890–1983), die unter dem Pseudo-
nym David Forme eine Reihe von Kriminalromanen um die beiden Figu-
ren verfasste. | 11 **to fool:** täuschen, reinlegen. | 13 **to cut in on s.o.:** jdn.
unterbrechen.

ment that he killed the King," she said. "I don't think the Macbeth woman was mixed up in it, either. You suspect them the most, of course, but those are the ones that are never guilty – or shouldn't be, anyway." "I'm afraid," I began, "that I –" "But don't you see?" said the American lady. "It would spoil everything if you could figure out right away who did it. Shakespeare was too smart for that. I've read that people never *have* figured out 'Hamlet,' so it isn't likely Shakespeare would have made 'Macbeth' as simple as it seems." I thought this over while I filled my pipe. "Who do you suspect?" I asked, suddenly. "Macduff," she said, promptly. "Good God!" I whispered, softly.

"Oh, Macduff did it, all right," said the murder specialist. "Hercule Poirot would have got him easily." "How did you figure it out?" I demanded. "Well," she said, "I didn't right away. At first I suspected Banquo. And then, of course, he was the second person killed. That was good right in there, that part. The person you suspect of the first murder should always be the second victim." "Is that so?" I murmured. "Oh, yes," said my informant. "They have to keep surprising you. Well, after the second murder I didn't know *who* the killer was for a while." "How about Malcolm and Donalbain, the King's sons?" I asked. "As I remember it, they fled right after the first murder. That looks suspicious." "Too suspicious," said the American lady. "Much too suspicious. When they flee, they're never guilty. You can count on that." "I believe," I said, "I'll have a brandy," and I summoned the waiter. My companion leaned toward me,

---

2 **to be mixed up in s.th.:** in etwas involviert sein. | 24 **to flee:** fliehen (*flee – fled – fled*). | 28 **to summon s.o.:** jdn. rufen, zu sich bestellen.

her eyes bright, her teacup quivering. "Do you know who discovered Duncan's body?" she demanded. I said I was sorry, but I had forgotten. "Macduff discovers it," she said, slipping into the historical present. "Then he comes running downstairs and shouts, 'Confusion has broke open the Lord's anointed temple' and 'Sacrilegious murder has made his masterpiece' and on and on like that." The good lady tapped me on the knee. "All that stuff was *rehearsed*," she said. "You wouldn't say a lot of stuff like that, offhand, would you – if you had found a body?" She fixed me with a glittering eye. "I – " I began. "You're right!" she said. "You wouldn't! Unless you had practiced it in advance. 'My God, there's a body in here!' is what an innocent man would say." She sat back with a confident glare.

I thought for a while. "But what do you make of the Third Murderer?" I asked. "You know, the Third Murderer has puzzled 'Macbeth' scholars for three hundred years." "That's because they never thought of Macduff," said the American lady. "It was Macduff, I'm certain. You couldn't have one of the victims murdered by two ordinary thugs – the murderer always has to be somebody important." "But what about the banquet scene?" I asked, after a moment.

---

1 **to quiver:** zittern. | 6 **anointed:** gesalbt. Die Amerikanerin verwechselt den Wortlaut des Ausrufs: »Confusion now hath made his masterpiece. / Most sacrilegious murder hath broke ope / The Lord's anointed temple« (*Macbeth* II,3,66–68). | 8 **to tap:** klopfen. | **rehearsed:** hier: vorbereitet, einstudiert. | 9 **offhand:** aus dem Stand. | 14 **glare:** penetranter Blick. | 16 **Third Murderer:** Über die Identität des dritten Mörders, der sich in *Macbeth* III,3 zu den zwei von Macbeth bestellten Mördern gesellt, um Banquo und dessen Sohn zu töten, hat die Shakespeare-Forschung lange spekuliert. | 20 **thug:** Rüpel. | 22 **banquet scene:** *Macbeth* III,4. In dieser Szene erscheint Macbeth der Geist des ermordeten Banquo.

"How do you account for Macbeth's guilty actions there, when Banquo's ghost came in and sat in his chair?" The lady leaned forward and tapped me on the knee again. "There wasn't any ghost," she said. "A big, strong man like that doesn't go around seeing ghosts – especially in a brightly lighted banquet hall with dozens of people around. Macbeth was *shielding somebody*!" "Who was he shielding?" I asked. "Mrs. Macbeth, of course," she said. "He thought she did it and he was going to take the rap himself. The husband always does that when the wife is suspected." "But what," I demanded, "about the sleepwalking scene, then?" "The same thing, only the other way around," said my companion. "That time *she* was shielding *him*. She wasn't asleep at all. Do you remember where it says, 'Enter Lady Macbeth with a taper'?" "Yes," I said. "Well, people who walk in their sleep *never carry lights*!" said my fellow-traveler. "They have a second sight. Did you ever hear of a sleepwalker carrying a light?" "No," I said, "I never did." "Well, then, she wasn't asleep. She was acting guilty to shield Macbeth." "I think," I said, "I'll have another brandy," and I called the waiter. When he brought it, I drank it rapidly and rose to go. "I believe," I said, "that you have got hold of something. Would you lend me that 'Macbeth?' I'd like to look it over tonight. I don't feel, somehow, as if I'd ever really read it." "I'll get it for you," she said. "But you'll find that I am right."

---

7 **to shield:** beschützen. | 9 **to take the rap:** (fig.) den Kopf hinhalten. | 11 **sleepwalking scene:** In *Macbeth* V,1 tritt die verstörte Lady Macbeth schlafwandelnd auf. | 15 **taper:** Kerze.

I read the play over carefully that night, and the next morning, after breakfast, I sought out the American woman. She was on the putting green, and I came up behind her silently and took her arm. She gave an exclamation. "Could I see you alone?" I asked, in a low voice. She nodded cautiously and followed me to a secluded spot. "You've found out something?" she breathed. "I've found out," I said, triumphantly, "the name of the murderer!" "You mean it wasn't Macduff?" she said. "Macduff is an innocent of those murders," I said, "as Macbeth and the Macbeth woman." I opened the copy of the play, which I had with me, and turned to Act II, Scene 2. "Here," I said, "you will see where Lady Macbeth says, 'I laid their daggers ready. He could not miss 'em. Had he not resembled my father as he slept, I had done it.' Do you see?" "No," said the American woman, bluntly, "I don't." "But it's simple!" I exclaimed. "I wonder I didn't see it years ago. The reason Duncan resembled Lady Macbeth's father as he slept is that *it actually was her father*!" "Good God!" breathed my companion, softly. "Lady Macbeth's father killed the King," I said, "and, hearing someone coming, thrust the body under the bed and crawled into the bed himself." "But," said the lady, "you can't have a murderer who only appears in the story once. You can't have that." "I know that," I said, and I turned to Act II, Scene 4. "It says here, 'Enter Ross with an old Man.' Now, that old man is never identified and it is my contention he was old Mr. Macbeth, whose ambition it was to

---

3 **putting green:** Grün (letzter Abschnitt jeder Spielbahn eines Golfplatzes). | 6 **secluded:** abgeschieden, abgelegen. | 14 **to resemble s.o.:** jdm. ähneln. | 21 **to thrust:** schieben, stoßen.

make his daughter Queen. There you have your motive." "But even then," cried the American lady, "he's still a minor character!" "Not," I said, gleefully, "when you realize that he was also *one of the weird sisters in disguise!*" "You mean one of the three witches?" "Precisely," I said. "Listen to this speech of the old man's. 'On Tuesday last, a falcon towering in her pride of place, was by a mousing owl hawk'd and kill'd.' Who does that sound like?" "It sounds like the way the three witches talk," said my companion, reluctantly. "Precisely!" I said again. "Well," said the American woman, "maybe you're right, but – " "I'm sure I am," I said. "And do you know what I'm going to do now?" "No," she said. "What?" "Buy a copy of 'Hamlet,'" I said, "and solve *that!*" My companion's eye brightened. "Then," she said, "you don't think Hamlet did it?" "I am," I said, "absolutely positive he didn't." "But who," she demanded, "do you suspect?" I looked at her cryptically. "Everybody," I said, and disappeared into a small grove of trees as silently as I had come.

---

3 **gleefully:** ausgelassen. | 4 **weird sisters:** So nennen sich die Hexen in *Macbeth* I,3,30 (in den meisten Ausgaben: *Weïrd Sisters*) selbst (*weird*: seltsam, unheimlich; hier etwa: in übernatürlicher Weise mit dem Schicksal verbunden; von altengl. *wyrd* ›Schicksal‹). | 7 **to tower:** hier: segeln, gleiten. | 8 **hawk'd:** im Flug angegriffen. | 17 **cryptically:** kryptisch, geheimnisvoll, mysteriös. | 18 **grove:** Hain.

The Merchant of Venice, told by Lancelot Gobbo, Shylock's Servant
   by Humphrey Carpenter

   To Messrs Montague & Capulet
   Bankers
   Verona

Gentlemen,
I beg to enquire whether there is any chance of obtaining employment in your office. For the past five years I have held a responsible position in the distinguished Venetian merchant banking house of Shylock & Shylock, but circumstances now make it necessary for me to seek a new post.

The bank's chairman, Mr Shylock, has recently undergone a business misfortune which has obliged him to cease trading, under somewhat distressing circumstances. (Please pardon the smudge in the above sentence. It occurred when the bailiffs carelessly knocked over my ink bottle while throwing me out into the street, along with Mr Shylock's few remaining items of property.)

Our chairman's judgement of credit-worthiness in the bank's clients was always faultless, and no one in the Vene-

---

4 **Messrs:** Abk. für den Plural von *Mr.* | **Montague & Capulet:** Namen der zerstrittenen Familien in *Romeo and Juliet*. | 8 **to beg** (poet.): um Erlaubnis bitten. | **to obtain:** bekommen, erhalten. | 10 **distinguished:** angesehen, ausgezeichnet. | 13 **post:** Posten, Arbeitsstelle. | 15 **to oblige s.o. to do s.th.:** jdn. zwingen, etwas zu tun. | **to cease doing s.th.:** aufhören etwas zu tun. | 16 **distressing:** schmerzlich. | 17 **smudge:** Fleck. | 18 **bailiff:** Gerichtsvollzieher. | 22 **faultless:** tadellos.

tian business world would have predicted that such a pillar of the financial community as Mr Antonio would default on the repayment of the substantial loan he had from us (this was on account of several cargo ships of his ownership all sinking at once).

The loss of the sum advanced to Mr Antonio would have been a small matter for our firm, had not our chairman agreed somewhat unusual terms with the client. This occasioned because the client, Mr Antonio, was in the deplorable habit of lending money to other members of the business community without charging interest, a practice which you will agree strikes at the heart of the financial world, especially at banking houses such as ourselves, which owe their very existence to realistic interest rates.

For his part, Mr Antonio claimed to deplore professional "money-lending" (a crude term he chose to use for merchant banking), and only approached us for a loan because his cash-flow was temporarily impeded by business activities, and he wished to give financial assistance to a young friend, a Mr Bassanio. This gentleman needed the wherewithal to kit himself out for travelling to a country man-

---

1 **pillar:** hier (fig.): Säule. | 2 f. **to default on repayments:** mit Zahlungen in Verzug geraten. | 3 **substantial:** beträchtlich, erheblich. | **loan:** Darlehen. | 4 **of his ownership:** in seinem Besitz. | 6 **to advance a sum:** eine Summe vorstrecken. | 9 **to occasion** (poet., rare): sich ergeben. | 10 **deplorable:** erbärmlich, ungeheuerlich. | 11 **interest:** Zins(en). | 12 **to strike at the heart of s.th.:** ins Herz einer Sache treffen. | 16 **for his part:** seinerseits. | 19 **to impede s.th.:** etwas behindern. | 21 f. **wherewithal:** das nötige Kleingeld. | 22 **to kit o.s. out:** sich ausrüsten, ausstatten.

The Works   93

sion, Belmont, there to woo, in some style, the wealthy young lady of the house, a Miss Portia.

It was Miss Portia's habit to set a kind of party game for the young gentlemen who fancied her. She would put out three boxes, one made of gold, one of silver and one of lead, and tell them to guess which one contained her portrait. She believed that anyone who went for the gold or the silver must be after her money. Mr Bassanio sensibly chose the lead box, and acquired the lady. (This has nothing to do with my job application, gentlemen, and I apologize for straying from the matter in hand.) Meanwhile, Mr Antonio was in the unfortunate situation of realizing that he could not repay the loan, on account of his ships having sunk to the bottom of the sea.

This, it must be admitted, was exactly what our chairman had hoped would happen, as it allowed him to put into effect Clause 9(b), paragraph (3) of the loan agreement he had drawn up with Mr Antonio. This stated that, should the loan not be repaid, our chairman was entitled to cut off a piece of Mr Antonio's flesh, weighing 453.59 grams, or to use the old system of weights, one pound, this to be removed from any part of the client's body at our chairman's discretion.

This unusual agreement naturally caused something of a stir in the business community, especially when it became

---

1 **to woo s.o.:** jdn. umwerben. | 4 **to fancy s.o.:** jdn. attraktiv finden, auf jdn. scharf sein. | 5 **lead:** Blei. | 11 **to stray from s.th.:** von etwas abschweifen. | 17 **clause:** Klausel. | 18 **to draw up s.th.:** etwas (Vertrag) aufsetzen (*draw – drew – drawn*). | 23 **discretion:** Ermessen. | 24 f. **to cause a stir:** Aufsehen erregen.

known that the due date of repayment had passed without our chairman receiving Mr Antonio's cheque. It was announced that the legal proceedings were to be instituted at once by our chairman, so as to obtain the aforesaid 453.59 grams of Mr Antonio's flesh.

Miss Portia (or Mrs Bassanio as she had now become) took a keen interest in the financial world, being a lady of not inconsiderable means, and when she heard of these developments she and her personal assistant laid plans for (if you will pardon the expression) saving Mr Antonio's bacon, or at least 453.59 grams of it, seeing as how his predicament had arisen on account of his generosity to her husband.

She and the PA – a lady named Miss Nerissa, whom, I omitted to mention, had simultaneously become married to Mr Bassanio's companion, Mr Gratiano – set off for Venice without informing their husbands, and there managed to kit themselves out in lawyers' wigs and gowns, making out that they were, respectively, a distinguished barrister from Padua by the name of Mr Bellario, and his clerk. They then had themselves engaged as lawyers by Mr Antonio.

The following is a transcript of the court proceedings:

---

3 **to institute s.th.:** etwas einleiten. | 4 **aforesaid:** oben erwähnt, besagt. | 8 **not inconsiderable:** nicht unbeträchtlich. | 10 f. **to save s.o.'s bacon:** jdm. den Hals retten. | 11 f. **predicament** [prɪ'dɪkəmənt]: Notlage, Schwierigkeiten. | 12 **to arise:** entstehen, sich ergeben (*arise – arose – arisen*). | 14 **PA:** Abk. für *Personal Assistant*. | 20 **barrister:** Barrister (Rechtsanwalt bei den englischen Obergerichten). | 23 **court proceedings** (pl.): Gerichtsverfahren.

JUDGE. Now, er, Mr Shylock, this is all a jolly good joke, threatening to chop off a chap's whatsit – I imagine that's what you've got in mind, old chap?

MR SHYLOCK. Actually, no. His heart was the bit I'd got my eye on.

(*Commotion in court.*)

JUDGE. Well, a joke's a joke, but his friends have all rallied round and offered you twice the money, so why don't you take it and call the whole thing off?

MR SHYLOCK. Sorry, my lord, but a contract is a contract.

(*Looks around.*)

Has somebody sharpened that knife for me?

(*More commotion.*)

MR ANTONIO (*undoing his shirt*). It's a waste of time arguing. I know what these merchant bankers are. Let's get on with it.

(*Still more commotion.*)

MR BELLARIO (*counsel for Mr Antonio, getting to his feet*). If my client would allow me to conduct his case, I would venture to ask Mr Shylock if he might consider being merciful to my client?

MR SHYLOCK. No.

MR BELLARIO. I see. In that case, my client might as well get on with undoing the other buttons.

(*Even more commotion, and cries of "Antonio, get yourself a better lawyer!"*)

---

1 **jolly:** lustig. | 2 **whatsit:** Dings (gemeint ist: Penis). | 3 **old chap:** alter Freund, altes Haus. | 6 **commotion:** Aufruhr. | 7 f. **to rally round:** sich zusammentun. | 18 **counsel:** Anwalt, Verteidiger. | 19 **to conduct a case:** einen Prozess führen. | 21 **merciful:** gnädig.

MR SHYLOCK *(delighted)*. Excellent class of lawyer they're turning out from law school these days.

MR BELLARIO. Thank you. And as you will have noticed, I have here a very accurate weighing machine, to check that it's 453.59 grams you've cut off my client.

MR SHYLOCK. Fine, fine. *(Someone hands him the knife, and he tests it.)*

Just the job. Here we go then.

MR BELLARIO. Exactly 453.59 grams, mind you. That's what's written in the contract.

MR SHYLOCK *(slightly uneasily)*. Ah yes. Exactly 453 grams.

MR BELLARIO. No, exactly 453.59 grams. Not 0.60, or for that matter 0.58.

MR SHYLOCK *(sweating slightly)*. Well, I don't know I can get it quite as precisely as that. I mean, I'm not one of those microsurgeons. Can I put a bit back if I take too much?

MR BELLARIO. Not according to the contract.

MR SHYLOCK *(turning rather pale)*. Ah, I see.

MR BELLARIO. Well, it was you who drew up the contract, wasn't it? And, of course, no blood.

MR SHYLOCK *(loosening his collar)*. I beg your pardon?

MR BELLARIO. Not a drop of my client's blood may be shed. Not one single drop.

MR SHYLOCK. That is ridiculous. It says in the contract that I can cut this bit off him. How on earth am I supposed to do that without shedding blood?

MR BELLARIO. My dear Mr Shylock, you should have thought of that when you drew up the contract.

---

11 **uneasily:** beunruhigt, unbehaglich. | 24 **to shed s.th.:** etwas vergießen.

(Laughter in court.)

MR ANTONIO *(beaming)*. Excellent class of lawyer they're turning out from law school these days.

MR SHYLOCK. Er, my lord, I think I'll take the money after all.

MR BELLARIO. Sorry, Mr Shylock, but a contract is a contract.

(More laughter.)

Isn't that true, my lord?

JUDGE *(waking up)*. Whatever you say, Mr Bellario. I must confess this whole case is rather beyond me.

MR BELLARIO. But not beyond me, my lord. My client has already refused the offer of the money owed him, with the words "a contract is a contract". The contract obliges him to detach 453.58 –

EVERYONE IN COURT. 453.59.

MR BELLARIO. So sorry. *(Laughter.)* To detach 453.59 grams of my client's flesh, but *precisely* that amount, and without spilling even one milligram of blood. So, get on with it, Mr Shylock.

MR SHYLOCK *(gathering his papers and putting away the knife)*. My lord must be aware that counsel for Mr Antonio is asking the impossible. If Mr Antonio will repay me the sum I lent him, without interest, I shall be content to drop the matter.

(Cheers in court.)

MR BELLARIO. But I will not. By declaring his intention to cut this piece from the region of my client's heart, Mr

---

11 **is rather beyond me:** kapiere ich nicht. | 15 **to detach:** abtrennen.

Shylock has, in effect, announced his intention of killing him. Do you agree, my lord?

JUDGE *(waking up again)*. Er, well, I suppose so, yes.

MR BELLARIO. And you know the penalty for that, my lord, under Venetian law?

JUDGE. Well, er, I can't call it to mind right now.

MR BELLARIO. The penalty, my lord, is that anyone the courts find guilty of plotting to kill someone must give up half of his wealth to his intended victim …

MR SHYLOCK. Strewth! Well, at least it's only half.

MR BELLARIO. … and half to the government.

MR SHYLOCK *(gulping)*. Do you mind if I sit down? Not feeling very well.

MR ANTONIO. I don't want half his goods; I'll settle for a quarter, and when I die I'll leave it to the chap who recently eloped with his daughter.

(Antonio is carried shoulder high out of the court, to shouts of "For he's a jolly good fellow". Mr Shylock is smuggled through the crowd in a blanket.)

When it was discovered that "Mr Bellario" was in fact a lady completely without legal qualifications, there was some call for the case to come to court again, but by that time our chairman had slipped away from Venice with a number of clients' funds. Despite repeated reports of sightings in the newspapers, the international police have not been able to trace him.

---

4 **penalty:** Strafe. | 9 **intended:** vorgesehen. | 10 **strewth:** wow! (aus *God's truth*). | 16 **to elope with s.o.:** mit jdm. weglaufen, durchbrennen. | 23 **to slip away:** sich davonschleichen, sich wegstehlen.

The Works

I am consequently out of a job, and am thinking of moving to Verona, where I gather the pace of life in the business world is somewhat quieter. I am sure, gentlemen, that rumours which have reached Venice, about the heads of your firm, Mr Montague and Mr Capulet, falling out with each other, are considerably exaggerated.

I look forward to your prompt reply.

Yours sincerely,
L. Gobbo (Mr)

The Sonnets[17]

I

The expense of spirits is a crying shame,
So is the cost of wine. What bard today
Can live like old Khayyám? It's not the same –
A loaf and Thou and Tesco's Beaujolais.
I had this bird called Sharon, fond of gin –
Could knock back six or seven. At the price

---

17 These are parodies of Shakespeare's sonnets 129 and 14 by Wendy Cope.

5f. **to fall out with s.o.:** sich mit jdm. zerstreiten. | 14 **Khayyám:** Omar K. (1048–1131), persischer Dichter. | 15 **A loaf and Thou and Tesco's Beaujolais:** Anspielung auf das berühmteste Zitat aus der Gedichtsammlung *The Rubáiyát of Omar Khayyám*: »A Jug of Wine, a Loaf of Bread and Thou« (übers. von Edward FitzGerald). | 16 **bird** (coll.): Tussi, Mieze. | 17 **to knock back s.th.:** etwas (alkoholisches Getränk) hinunterkippen.

I paid a high wage for each hour of sin
And that was why I only had her twice.
Then there was Tracy, who drank rum and Coke,
So beautiful I didn't mind at first
But love grows colder. Now some other bloke
Is subsidizing Tracy and her thirst.
I need a woman, honest and sincere,
Who'll come across on half a pint of beer.

II

Not from the stars do I my judgement pluck,
Although I often read my horoscope.
Today *The Standard* promises me luck
With money and with girls. One can but hope.
Astrologers may not know if you'll win
The football pools or when you'll get a screw,
But one thing's clearer than this glass of gin –
Their character analyses are true.
Cancerians are sympathetic, kind,
Intuitive, creative, sentimental,
Exceptionally shrewd and, you will find,
They make fantastic lovers, warm and gentle.
Amazing, really, that you fail to see
How very well all this applies to me.

---

5 **bloke:** Kerl, Typ. | 6 **to subsidize s.o.:** jdn. bezuschussen. | 8 **to come across:** etwa: willig, gefügig werden. | 10 **to pluck:** pflücken. | 15 **football pools** (pl.): Fußballtoto. | **to get a screw:** eine Frau rumkriegen; (vulg.): vögeln. | 18 **Cancerian** [kæn'seəriən]: Krebs (Astrologie). | 20 **shrewd:** schlau, gewieft.

XVIII *(in Klingon)*

> "You have not experienced Shakespeare until you have read him in the original Klingon."
> High Chancellor Gorkon, Star Trek VI: *The Undiscovered Country*

High Chancellor Gorkon is right: the English translations of Shakespeare's Klingon poetry are but a weak imitation of the original. Experiencing Shakespeare in the original Klingon *is* possible, however. *Much Ado About Nothing* is available under its original title *paghmo' tln mlS*, and so is *Hamlet*, with its famous soliloquy "taH pagh taHbe'". Here is Sonnet XVIII:

qaDelmeH bov tuj pem vIlo'choHQo'.
SoH 'IH 'ej belmoH law', oH belmoH puS.
jar vagh tIpuq DIHo'bgh Sang Sus ro'.
'ej ratlhtaHmeH bov tuj leSpoH luvuS.

rut tujqu' bochtaHvIS chal mIn Dun qu'.
rut DotlhDaj SuD wov HurghmoHmeH, HuvHa'.
'ej reH Hoch 'IHvo' Sab Hoch 'IH, net tu'.
'u' He choHmo', San njochmo' joq quvHa'.

'ach not wovHa'choH jubbogh bovlIj tuj,
'ej not ghomHa'choH Hochvetlh 'IH Daghajbogh,
'ej "QIbwIjDaq bIleng" not mIy Hegh nuj,
bovmey DaDontaHvIS, DojwI' nIHajbogh!

---

1 **Klingon:** Sprache der Klingonen, einer außerirdischen Spezies in den *Star Trek*-Filmen.

tlhuHlaH 'ej legh, wej 'e' lumevchugh nuv,
vaj yIntaH bomvam, 'ej DuyInmoH quv.

Hamlet on Film

If you are making a film version of *Hamlet*, especially in another language, then it seems you have to make the film sound a bit more exciting by changing the title …

Hamlet, Scène de Duel (1900, France)
Être Ou Être Pas (1914, France)
A sagebrush Hamlet (1919, Western, USA)
Hamlet at Elsinore (1951, Ireland)
Der Rest ist Schweigen (1959, Germany)
Inmolación de Hamlet (1967, Spain, "The Sacrifice of Hamlet")
Ofelias Blomsters (1968, Denmark, "Ophelia's Flowers")
H for Hamlet (1993, Ireland)

---

9 **sagebrush:** Wüstensalbei, typisch für die Landschaft in Westernfilmen.

Shakespeare – the Rude Bits

> Shakespeare should not be put into the hands of the young
> without the warning that the foolish things in his plays were
> written to please the foolish, the filthy for the filthy, and the
> brutal for the brutal [...].
> Robert Bridges[18]

Let us start with a common misconception:

Shakespeare used sexual language to please the groundlings.

The main reason this is a misconception is that a lot of people don't know who the groundlings were. So: who were the groundlings? The groundlings were those people who frequented the 'ground' or pit of a theatre. They were people of average or inferior taste, uncritical and unrefined, and possibly ugly and smelly as well. As a groundling, you paid only a penny to go to the theatre, but you got wet, and it stank, and there was a danger of being robbed. On the positive side, you got a close-up view of the action, and you could also buy food and drink. Because Hamlet mentions the groundlings ("O, it offends me to the soul to hear a robustious, periwig-pated fellow tear a passion to tatters, to very rags, to split the ears of the groundlings, who for the

---

18 Robert Bridges, "The Influence of the Audience on Shakespeare's Drama", in: R. B., *Collected Essays, Papers Etc.*, Vol. 1, Oxford: Oxford University Press, 1927, p. 28.

---

4 **filthy:** schmutzig. | 7 **misconception:** Irrglaube. | 13 **to frequent:** (häufig) besuchen. | 14 **inferior:** minderwertig. | **unrefined:** unkultiviert. | 21 **periwig-pated:** eine Perücke tragend.

most part are capable of nothing but inexplicable dumb shows and noise", III,2,11) they have acquired a special status in Shakespeare scholarship.

There is no doubt that Shakespeare is filthy, rude, obscene, and indecent. And it seems possible that the 'groundlings' appreciated these bits more than other members of the audience. Another way of explaining the rude bits, however, is to say that Shakespeare had nothing to do with it. According to this theory, the rude bits were invented by actors (this is what the English poet Alexander Pope thought in 1725). They certainly did not come from the delicate and refined throat of the Swan of Avon. In the 19th century, the vulgar passages were found to be so offensive that Henrietta and Thomas Bowdler simply removed anything they thought was indecent or profane. The result was not only a "Family Shakspeare"(1807 – you can see Bowdler didn't know how to spell Shakespeare), but also a new word. Since then, 'bowdlerize' means to remove offensive elements from a text.

The Taming of the Screw, As You Lick It,[19] *Much Ado About Humping* – some film producers have gone to great lengths to make the Bard rude, but they needn't have both-

---

19 Fans of the US animated sitcom *The Simpsons* may know that "As You Lick It" is also the name of an ice-cream parlour in Springfield.

1f. **dumb show:** Pantomime. | 5 **indecent:** ungehörig. | 14 **Henrietta and Thomas Bowdler:** Thomas B. (1754–1825), Arzt und Literat. Bowdlers unverheiratete Schwester Henrietta (1750–1830) wurde auf dem Titelblatt der *Family Shakspeare* nicht erwähnt, damit ihr Ruf nicht darunter leidet. | 20f. **screw / humping** (vulg.): Geschlechtsverkehr.

ered. Shakespeare *is* rude. And the rudest thing about Shakespeare, according to leading Shakespeare scholars, is his name: Shakespeare's name itself is an obscenity. After all, it refers to the shaking of a spear. A spear obviously has phallic properties.[20] So Shakespeare himself was obviously, well, a wanker. And his first name – in the abbreviated form 'Will' – was not only a pun on sexual desire, but also on 'penis' and 'vagina'. Poor Will Shakespeare! People must have made fun of him all the time!

What is 'bawdy'?
When talking about obscenity and vulgarity in Shakespeare, there is a very important word: 'bawdy'. Generations of Shakespeare editors have referred to 'bawdy puns', 'bawdy quibbles' or simply to 'bawdy' in the plays. What do they mean?

If we want to know what 'bawdy' means, the best place to start is to ask that naughtiest, perhaps most sexual of all Shakespeare's characters, Mercutio from *Romeo and Juliet*, who talks about the "bawdy hand of the dial" being "upon the prick of noon" (II,4,104 f.). This is a 'quibble', or a play on words: 'hand' and 'prick' both have two meanings here. And it is a 'bawdy quibble', because it is lewd, rude, vulgar, indecent and obscene. Fancy another bawdy quibble? In

---

20 Things like this are more obvious to some people than to others.

---

5 **properties:** Eigenschaften. | 6 **wanker:** Wichser. | 11 **vulgarity:** Vulgarität. | 14 **quibble:** Wortspiel. | 20 **prick** (vulg.): Schwanz. | 22 **lewd:** obszön, unanständig. | 23 **Fancy ...:** hier: Möchten Sie ... ? (*to fancy s.th.:* Lust auf etwas haben, etwas mögen).

The Two Gentlemen of Verona the two servants Lance and Speed are conversing about how things are between Julia and Proteus:

> SPEED. Why then, how stands the matter with them?
> LANCE. Marry, thus: when it stands well with him it stands well with her.   (II,5,19–21)

It is clear what Launce means by "it stands"; Speed, however, doesn't seem to understand what is 'standing' and answers "What an ass art thou! I understand thee not". And it is certain the uncouth members of the audience would have had a good laugh about this. So, in summary, Shakespeare's bawdy quibbles were primarily for the groundlings.

How to spell the rudest word in the English language

It is true that the most obscene word in the English language never occurs in Shakespeare's plays, but he certainly knew how to spell it. In *Twelfth Night*, Malvolio, a vain puritan bore, receives a letter he thinks is from his beloved Olivia (it is actually from someone else who is trying to make a fool of him). He recognises – and describes – her handwriting:

> By my life, this is my lady's hand. These be her very c's, her u's, and her t's, and thus makes she her great P's.
> *Twelfth Night* II,5,84–87

---

2 **to converse:** sich unterhalten. | 10 **uncouth:** ungehobelt, grob. | 17 **vain:** eitel. | 17f. **puritan:** puritanisch. | 18 **bore:** Langweiler.

Without realising it (and with the help of the word 'and', which would sound like 'en'), Malvolio has spelled a four-letter word that was as popular – and as taboo – then as it is now. To cap things off, he adds that she "makes her great P's".

How to say F--- off!
For a long time, Shakespeare scholars weren't willing to accept that Hamlet uses language to refer to bawdiness. In the first scene of the third act Hamlet tells Ophelia to go to a "nunnery". In Shakespeare's time, this was another word for 'brothel'. So in effect, Hamlet is telling Ophelia to "F--- off!" And it seems certain that he is being indecent in the following dialogue with Ophelia (III,2,107-116):

HAMLET. Lady, shall I lie in your lap?
OPHELIA. No, my lord.
HAMLET. I mean my head upon your lap?
OPHELIA. Ay, my lord.
HAMLET. Do you think I meant country matters?
OPHELIA. I think nothing, my lord.
HAMLET. That's a fair thought to lie between maids' legs.
OPHELIA. What is, my lord?
HAMLET. No thing.
OPHELIA. You are merry, my lord.

This seems harmless enough. But what Hamlet really means is this:

---

4 **to cap things off**: und um den Ganzen die Krone aufzusetzen, zur Krönung. | 10 **nunnery**: (Nonnen-)Kloster. | 11 **brothel**: Bordell.

108   Shakespeare – the Rude Bits

HAMLET. Lady, shall I ▮▮▮ in your ▮▮▮?
OPHELIA. No, my lord.
HAMLET. I mean the tip of my ▮▮▮ upon your ▮▮▮?
OPHELIA. Yes, my lord.
HAMLET. Do you think I was referring to matters concerning the ▮▮▮?
OPHELIA. I think about a ▮▮▮ my lord.
HAMLET. That's a fair thought – to ▮▮▮ between maids' legs.
OPHELIA. What is, my lord?
HAMLET. The ▮▮▮.
OPHELIA. You are horny, my lord.

What, you might ask, is so offensive about the word 'nothing'. 'Nothing' was slang for female genitalia. Maybe this is the reason King Charles I changed the title of *Much Ado About Nothing* to *Benedick and Beatrice*?

Sexy Sonnets
Many of the sonnets are about sex. There is no doubt about it. Here is sonnet 129, followed by a 'translation':

Th'expense of spirit in a waste of shame
Is lust in action; and till action, lust
Is perjured, murd'rous, bloody, full of blame,
Savage, extreme, rude, cruel, not to trust,
Enjoyed no sooner but despisèd straight,
Past reason hunted, and no sooner had

---

22 **perjured:** meineidig. | 24 **despisèd:** verachtet.

Shakespeare – the Rude Bits 109

Past reason hated as a swallowed bait
On purpose laid to make the taker mad;
Mad in pursuit and in possession so,
Had, having, and in quest to have, extreme;
A bliss in proof and proved, a very woe;
Before, a joy proposed; behind, a dream.
    All this the world well knows, yet none knows well
    To shun the heaven that leads men to this hell.

Sex is really just about having an orgasm. And before you have your way with a woman, lust makes you tell her you love her even though you don't. Lust and desire make you savage, violent, brutal, cruel; it means you can't be trusted.
As soon as you have had sex, you regret what you've done. It's crazy. And there's no reason why you should hate yourself for satisfying your lust. It's like bait that's put out on purpose to make the swallower mad with desire.
You nearly go crazy running after women, and when you have them, you go crazy anyway.
Having sex is fun, but when it's over you feel terrible. It's a joy to look forward to having sex, but afterwards, it's just a fleeting moment that means nothing.
Everyone knows this, of course, but no man is wise enough to stay away from women.

Sonnet 151 is all about having an erection. "An erect penis has no conscience", it seems to say.

---

1 **bait:** Köder. | 5 **bliss:** Wonne. | **woe:** Kummer, Leid. | 8 **to shun:** meiden. | 22 **fleeting:** flüchtig.

Love is too young to know what conscience is,
Yet who knows not conscience is born of love?
Then, gentle cheater, urge not my amiss,
Lest guilty of my faults thy sweet self prove.
For, thou betraying me, I do betray
My nobler part to my gross body's treason.
My soul doth tell my body that he may
Triumph in love; flesh stays no farther reason,
But rising at thy name doth point out thee
As his triumphant prize. Proud of this pride,
He is contented thy poor drudge to be,
To stand in thy affairs, fall by thy side.
  No want of conscience hold it that I call
  Her "love" for whose dear love I rise and fall.

There seems to be little doubt that con-science is a pun on the French con (cunt), so that the poet is toying with the idea of 'cunt-knowledge'. The poet, as the Shakespeare scholar Stanley Wells has noted, is nothing but a "rising and falling penis".[21]

75 Words Shakespeare used for sex[22]
act action activity acture angling back-trick banquet boarding bout broach buckle business caper colt conflict conver-

---

21 Stanley Wells, *Shakespeare, Sex, and Love*, Oxford: Oxford University Press, 2010, p. 46.
22 The following three word lists are drawn from Michael LoMonico, *The Shakespeare Book of Lists*, Franklin Lakes (N.J.): Career Press, 2001, p. 78f.

3 **amiss:** Fehler, Vergehen. | 11 **drudge:** Sklave, Diener. | 16 **cunt** (vulg.): Möse.

sation copulation couch cover custom deal deed die embalming encounter execution feat ferret fill foining foot game grinding groping hack horsemanship husbandry incorporate juggling kiss labour lay leap meddle mount night-work occupy play plough pop pray put to rite score shake sluice soil spend sport stuff take tasts thresh thrust tick-tack tillage top trick trim tumble tup union voyage wanton work

70 words Shakespeare used for male genitalia
apricot arm awl bauble beef bolt brand bugle carrot club cock codpiece dart distaff eel fiddle finger flesh hand holy-thistle hook horn instrument jack joint key knife lag end lance limb little finger loins member needle nose organ pear pen pike pin pipe pistol pizzle point pole poll-axe potato-finger prick privates R Roger root runnion shaft shake spirit stake stalk standard stump sword tale talent thing thorn three-inch fool tool weapon worm yard

70 words Shakespeare used for female genitalia
baldrick bay belly bird's nest bog boots bottle box breach buckles case chamber chink circle cistern city clack-dish cleft cliff commodity common place constable country crack den dial ell et cetera eye flower fountain furred pack gap garland gate glove hell hole hook jerkin lap lock mark medlar mouth nest Netherlands nothing O oven pit place plum pond quaint ring rose rudder ruff scut seat Spain sty tail thing treasure way well wound

Performing Shakespeare

> No one can convince me Shakespeare didn't make up words just to upset the actors.
> Jack Lemmon

> You can't improvise this shit!
> Dustin Hoffman, on iambic pentameter.

Blank Verse – Its usefulness ...

Blank verse is probably the very centre of Elizabethan tradition and perhaps the most important thing in Shakespeare that an actor has to come to terms with. Or rather I should say that an actor *needs to get help from*. I stress that because many actors, particularly if they're not familiar with Shakespeare, very understandably look at the verse as some kind of threat. They know they will somehow come to grief if they ignore it or be chastised if they do it wrong. It becomes a mountain to be climbed or else an obstacle to be avoided. But no, it's there to help the actor. It's full of little hints from Shakespeare about how to act a given speech or scene. It's stage-direction in shorthand.[23]

23 John Barton, *Playing Shakespeare*, London: Methuen, 1984, ch. 2, p. 25.

4 **Lemmon:** Jack L., d.i. J. Uhler (1925–2001), amerikanischer Schauspieler; bekannt vor allem für seine komischen Rollen. | 6 **Hoffman:** Dustin H. (geb. 1937), amerikanischer Schauspieler; hat 1989 in London den Shylock gespielt. | 10 **to come to terms with s.th.:** mit etwas zurechtkommen. | 14 **threat:** Bedrohung. | 14 f. **to come to grief:** scheitern. | 15 **to chastise s.o.:** jdn. rügen. | 16 **obstacle:** Hindernis. | 18 **hint:** Hinweis, Tipp. | 19 **shorthand:** Kurzschrift.

... and how to master it.

The Verse Problem – And How to Master It
by Patrick Barlow

Many a mickle makes a muckle.
   (Jonson & Johnson)

Introduction
Which brings us to one of the most critical problems for the Shakespearean actor. Namely, the verse problem.
So how do we master the verse problem and more to the point what is the verse problem?

The Verse Problem
Unfortunately nobody is quite sure what the Verse Problem is exactly, which makes "Mastering the Verse Problem" a slightly trickier 'nut to crack' than it would be if we did obviously. Suffice it to say, however, that it causes havoc in numerous regional and West End theatres and can usually be spotted by a number of 'tell-tale symptoms' such as con-

---

4 **Many a mickle makes a muckle** (prov.): Auch Kleinvieh macht Mist. | 5 **Jonson & Johnson:** Anspielung auf Ben Jonson (1572–1637) und Dr Samuel Johnson (1709–1784), englische Dichter; in der Doppelung auch Anspielung auf den amerikanischen Industriekonzern Johnson & Johnson. | 14 **nut to crack:** (fig.) harte Nuss. | 15 **suffice it to say:** es genügt wohl, wenn ich sage, dass … | **havoc:** Chaos, Durcheinander. | 16 **West End theatre:** Im Westen Londons befindet sich das Einkaufs- und Unterhaltungsviertel. | 17 **tell-tale:** verräterisch. | 17 f. **contrapuntal:** kontrapunktisch.

trapuntal off-beats, dissonant rhyming mechanisms, alliterative assonants and, worst of all, irregular vowel movements, which can cause serious, not to say agonising, problems for the emergent actor.*

Here anyway are some "Useful Exercises when Attempting Verse" which I have personally found extremely helpful.

Some Useful Exercises when Attempting Verse
1. Keep calm.
2. Lie on the floor and take three deep breaths followed by 149 short breaths without pause for three hours.
3. Shake out ankles, rib cage and lower intestine and above all – *relax*! And finally:
4. Good luck!

Shakespeare Masterclass
  by Stephen Fry and Hugh Laurie

DIRECTOR. All right, let's start at the beginning shall we?
ACTOR. Right, yeh.
DIRECTOR. What's the word, what's the word, I wonder, that Shakespeare decides to begin his sentence with here?
ACTOR. Er, "Time" is the first word.

* Not surprisingly.

---

1 **off-beats:** unbetonte Silben. | 1f. **alliterative:** alliterierend. | 2 **assonants:** Assonanzen (Gleichklänge). | 2f. **irregular vowel movements:** Wortspiel mit *irregular bowel movements* (pl.) ›Durchfall‹ (*bowel:* Gedärm). | 4 **emergent:** aufstrebend. | 12 **lower intestine:** Dickdarm.

DIRECTOR. Time, Time.

ACTOR. Yep.

DIRECTOR. And how does Shakespeare decide to spell it, Hugh?

ACTOR. T-I-M-E.

DIRECTOR. T-I?

ACTOR. M.

DIRECTOR. M-E.

ACTOR. Yep.

DIRECTOR. And what sort of spelling of the word is that?

ACTOR. Well it's the ordinary spelling.

DIRECTOR. It's the *ordinary* spelling, isn't it? It's the *conventional* spelling. So why out of all the spellings he could have chosen, did Shakespeare choose that one, do you think?

ACTOR. Well, um, because it gives us time in an ordinary sense.

DIRECTOR. Exactly, well done, good boy. Because it gives us time in an ordinary, conventional sense.

ACTOR. Oh, right.

DIRECTOR. So, Shakespeare has given us time in a conventional sense. But he's given us something else, Hugh. Have a look at the typography. What do you spy?

ACTOR. Oh. It's got a capital T.

DIRECTOR. Shakespeare's T is very much upper case, there, Hugh, isn't it? Why?

ACTOR. 'Cos it's the first word in the sentence.

---

4 **Hugh:** Die Skizze wurde erstmals von Stephen Fry und Hugh Laurie aufgeführt. | 23 **to spy:** erspähen. | 25 **very much:** im hohen Grade. | **upper case:** Großbuchstaben.

DIRECTOR. Well I think that's *partly* it. But I think there's another reason too. Shakespeare has given us time in a *conventional* sense – and time in an *abstract* sense.

ACTOR. Right, yes.

DIRECTOR. All right? Do you think your voice can convey that, Hugh?

ACTOR. I hope so.

DIRECTOR. I hope so too. All right. Give it a go.

ACTOR. Just the one word?

DIRECTOR. Just the one word for the moment.

ACTOR. Yep. *(He howls the word.)* TIME!

DIRECTOR. Wo, wo, wo. Where do we gather from?

ACTOR. Oh, the buttocks.

DIRECTOR. Always the buttocks. Gather from the buttocks. Thank you.

ACTOR *(gathering)*. Time!

DIRECTOR. Well, there are a number of things I liked about that, Hugh, there was ... there was ... there was a number of things I liked about that. All right, try it again, and this time try and bring in a sense of Troy falling, a sense of ruin, of folly, of anger, of decay, of hopelessness and despair, a sense of greed –

ACTOR. Ambition?

DIRECTOR. No, leave ambition out for the moment if you would, Hugh, of greed, or mortality, and of transience.

---

5 **to convey s.th.:** etwas vermitteln, deutlich werden lassen. | 12 **wo:** *whoa:* brr!; hier etwa: langsam! | **to gather from s.th.:** hier: Kräfte aus etwas sammeln. | 13 **buttocks** (pl.): Gesäß. | 20 **Troy falling:** die Einnahme Trojas. | 21 **ruin:** hier etwa: Untergang. | **folly:** Torheit. | **decay:** Verfall. | 25 **mortality:** Sterblichkeit. | **transience:** Vergänglichkeit.

All right? And try to suffuse the whole thing with a red colour ...
ACTOR. Time!
DIRECTOR. What went wrong there, Hugh?
ACTOR. I don't know. I got a bit lost in the middle actually.

A Tale of Revenge from *Macbeth*
by Derek Nimmo

Among Sir Donald Wolfit's touring company was a young actor whose aspirations sadly outstripped his ability. Wolfit cast him as Seyton in *Macbeth*, entrusting him with the news of Lady Macbeth's demise: "The queen, my lord, is dead." He played this for several seasons until it started to bore him and he asked Wolfit for a larger part. Wolfit declined. The actor continued asking and Wolfit stuck to his guns. Into this stalemate came thoughts of revenge. When *Macbeth* was next performed he ran on stage as usual and in answer to Macbeth's question, "Wherefore was that cry?" answered, "My lord, the queen is much better and is even now at dinner."

---

1 **to suffuse:** erfüllen. | 8 **Wolfit:** Sir Donald W. (1902–68), britischer Schauspieler und Theatermanager; wurde einer breiten Öffentlichkeit vor allem durch seine reisende Theatertruppe bekannt, bei der er in der Regel selbst die Hauptrolle übernahm. | 9 **to outstrip s.th.:** etwas übertreffen. | 10 **to cast s.o. as ...:** jdm. die Rolle des ... geben. | 11 **demise:** Untergang. | 14 f. **to stick to one's guns:** auf seinem Standpunkt beharren. | 15 **stalemate:** Patt.

Shakespeare in the Classroom

The following exam papers are intended for classroom use. They have been developed according to the latest pedagogical methods.

A. *Coming to terms with Shakespeare's vocabulary*

1. Write an essay describing what you would do with any THREE of the following:

   a) ouphes
   b) statute caps
   c) woosel
   d) vantbrace.[24]

2. Describe Shakespeare's use of vocabulary in the following quote:

   Is not a buff jerkin a most sweet robe of durance?
   (*1 Henry IV*, I,2,42 f.)

3. "Who would fardels bear?" asks Hamlet in his famous soliloquy "to be, or not to be". What is the best way to bear a fardel? Would you bear a fardel? If so, what is the maximum number of fardels you would bear?

---

24 Patrick Barlow, *Shakespeare: The Truth*, London: Methuen, 1983, ch. 28, p. 150.

---

16 **fardel:** Last, Bündel. | 17 **soliloquy** [sə'lɪlɪkwi]: Monolog.

B. *Othello*

Read *Othello* and then answer the following questions:

1. Are you too depressed, after reading this play, to answer questions on it?
2. Make a detailed comparison of the following speeches by Othello:
   a. "The handkerchief!"   (III,4,92)
   b. "The handkerchief!"   (III,4,93)
   c. "The handkerchief!"   (III,4,96)
3. "Her hand on her bosom, her head on her knee,
   Sing willow, willow, willow."
   Try singing *any* song in this position.
4. Was it tactful of Desdemona to say, in Othello's presence, that she was slain by "nobody"?
5. Considering all Iago did, including spreading lies, stealing handkerchiefs, getting people drunk, murdering, and inciting murder, don't you think there must be some easier way to become a lieutenant?[25]

[25] All five questions are to be found in Richard Armour, *Twisted Tales from Shakespeare*, New York: McGraw-Hill, 1957, p. 142.

---

11 **willow:** Weide (Baum). | 13 **tactful:** taktvoll. | 14 **to slay s.o.** (poet.): jdn. töten (*slay – slew – slain*). | 17 **to incite s.th.:** zu etwas anstiften.

C. *Hamlet*

Read *Hamlet* and then answer the following questions:

1. Have you noticed how, in Shakespeare's plays, when people said they saw a ghost they usually did? Were people more trustworthy in those days? Were ghosts?
2. Consider the effect on Ophelia's future if she had known how to swim.
3. Which is the most horrible line in the play? Not counting, of course, "O, horrible! O, horrible! Most horrible!" (I,5,80).
4. Would it give you comic relief to hold in your hands the skull of an old friend?
5. Don't you think Hamlet had rotten luck? In fact was anything more rotten in the state of Denmark?[26]

D. *Macbeth*

Read *Macbeth* and then answer the following questions:

1. Have you a weird sister? An odd brother?

---

26 For these five questions see Armour, p. 42.

---

5 **trustworthy:** vertrauenswürdig. | 11 **comic relief:** befreiende Komik. | 12 **skull:** Schädel. | 17 **weird:** seltsam, unheimlich; Anspielung auf die »Weird Sisters«, die Hexen aus *Macbeth* I,3,30; *weird* (bzw. *weïrd* in den meisten Shakespeare-Ausgaben) kommt von altengl. *wyrd* ›Schicksal‹, daher (fig.): in übernatürlicher Weise mit dem Schicksal verbunden.

2. Was Macbeth thane? How does he compare in this respect with Hamlet?
3. Would you trust Lady Macbeth as a wet nurse? Keep in mind her expression of solicitude for her own infant: "I would, while it was smiling in my face, have plucked my nipple from his boneless gums and dashed the brains out."
4. Which would you prefer in your stew:
   a. Newts' eyes?
   b. Dragons' scales?
   c. A dash of baboon blood?
5. "Upon my head," said Macbeth, "they placed a fruitless crown." What did he expect, a bowl of grapes and bananas?[27]

E. *The history plays*

Read the history plays (*The Life and Death of King John, The Life and Death of Richard the Second, The First Part of King Henry the Fourth, The Second Part of King Henry the Fourth, The Life of Henry the Fifth, The First Part of King Henry the Sixth, The Second Part of King Henry the Sixth, The Third Part of King Henry the Sixth, The Life and Death of Richard the Third, The Life of King Henry the Eighth*) and then answer the following question:

---

27 These questions are drawn from Armour, p. 63f.

1 **thane:** Gefolgsmann (Macbeth ist am Anfang des Dramas »Thane of Cawdor«); Wortspiel mit *sane* ›geistig gesund‹. | 3 **wet nurse:** Amme. | 4 **solicitude** [səˈlɪsɪtjuːd]: Fürsorge. | 5–7 **I Would ... the brains out:** *Macbeth* I,7,55–57. | 8 **stew:** Eintopf. | 9 **newt:** Molch. | 10 **scales:** (Fisch-)Schuppen. | 11 **babooon:** Pavian.

1. How did any *one* of the following differ from any one of the other?
   (1) *Henry IV Part 1*
   (2) *Henry IV Part 2*[28]

F. *Sonnets*

1. Put the sonnets in numerical order, starting at number one and ending with number 154.

Shakespeare's Age
   by Patrick Barlow
   "On us all doth haggish age creep on."
      (Shakespeare)

Introduction
So how should one begin with an examination of Shakespeare's age? And, more to the point, what exactly was it?

Shakespeare's Age
Unfortunately, it's a little difficult to know exactly how to give an answer to this rather odd question, but basically Shakespeare's age was Shakespeare's age. In other words, his aged changed from year to year, as everbody's age changes, i. e. we all have a different age depending on what year it is.

---

28 See W. C. Sellar and R. J. Yeatman, "From: 1066 and All That – Test Paper III", quoted from: *Everyman's Book of Nonsense*, edited by John Davies, London: Dent, 1981, p. 190.

10 **On us all ... creep on:** Anspielung auf *All's Well That Ends Well* I,2,29: »But on us both did haggish age steal on« (*haggish*: hässlich, abstoßend [*hag*: alte Frau]; *to steal on s.o.*: sich an jdn. heranschleichen).

Conclusion

In other words, to know how old anybody is all depends on what year you're talking about.

And Shakespeare was no exception.

THINGS TO DO:
1. Write short notes on the following: Shakespeare's Age.

Cooking with Shakespeare

What better way of becoming familiar with the Bard than trying to cook one of his recipes? We all know about Proust and his Madeleine cake,[29] but who has given any thought to Shakespeare's love of fine food and cookery?[30] It is a little-known fact that Shakespeare was a very good cook. His enthusiasm for working in kitchen is revealed in many of his plays, here for example in *Henry IV Part 2*:

> Some pigeons, Davy, a couple of short-legged hens, a joint of mutton, and any pretty little tiny kickshaws, tell William Cook.   (V,1,22–24)

"Tell William cook": these must have been familiar words to Shakespeare. A "kickshaw" is a fancy dish, so it seems certain that Shakespeare was a cook who liked to use food decoratively and creatively, which is hardly surprising, given the way he used language. And the following line from *Romeo and Juliet* makes it clear that he also saw cookery as a sensual activity:

> 'Tis an ill cook that cannot lick his own fingers.   (IV,2,6)

---

29 If you don't know about Proust and his Madeleine cake, all you need to know is that Madeleine did not survive the process.
30 I have.

---

10 **joint of mutton:** Hammelbraten.

It seems certain that Shakespeare was employed as a sous-chef at the exclusive THREE PIGEONS, during the Lost Years,[31] and it is obvious that Shakespeare's plays contain so many scenes of drinking and eating because he liked to prepare food for his actors. (Some scholars say he used food to characterize the people who populate the world of his plays, or that he uses food as a metaphor. What rubbish!) It is easy to imagine Shakespeare himself playing Macbeth on the stage of the Globe Theatre after a hard afternoon in the kitchen, raising his glass and saying:

> I drink to th' general joy of th'whole table.
> (*Macbeth* III,4,88)

We can imagine the festive table, on it the fine meats, salads and cakes the Bard had prepared just a few hours before. A close reading of Shakespeare's plays reveals that he was not only a good cook, but also a good judge of how much food to cook for his guests – always one of the most difficult parts of preparing a meal for visitors. Consider this passage from *Antony and Cleopatra*:

> Eight wild boars roasted whole at a breakfast and but twelve persons there. (II,2,186 f.)

---

[31] All evidence suggests that the Three Pigeons was not a pub, but rather a high-class restaurant. Shakespeare had ample opportunity to try new recipes here. See: *Shakespeare in the Kitchen. New Documents from the Lost Years*, Oxford 2013.

1 f. **sous-chef:** stellvertretender Küchenchef. | 2 f. **Lost Years:** Die Jahre 1585–92. | 6 **to populate:** bevölkern. | 23 f. **ample opportunity:** reichlich, jede Gelegenheit.

Here, Shakespeare is drawing our attention to the danger of letting people go hungry.

So, while the King's Men were busy working out how to perform his plays, Shakespeare was in the kitchen dicing carrots and plucking pheasants. Much has been made of Shakespeare's three roles – actor, playwright and shareholder – but it is time to add a fourth: he was also the in-house cook.

Filling your kitchen with the scents and smells of Elizabethan cookery is easier than you might think. With much Elizabethan cookery it is not so much the freshness of the ingredients, but their horribleness that is the key to the success of a particular dish. This is especially true of Shakespeare's most famous recipe. Here it is – with annotations and tips for successful cooking in the early 21st century. Bon appétit!

'More newts – Macbeth is staying to dinner.'

4 **to dice carrots:** Karotten in Würfel schneiden. | 5 **to pluck pheasants:** Fasanen rupfen. | 7 f. **in-house:** hauseigen. | 9 **scent:** Duft.

Potage Macbethienne[32]

> Round about the cauldron go,
> In the poisoned entrails throw.
> Toad, that under cold stone
> Days and nights has thirty-one
> Sweltered venom sleeping got,
> Boil thou first i'th' charmèd pot.
> Fillet of a fenny snake,
> In the cauldron boil and bake.
> Eye of newt and toe of frog,
> Wool of bat and tongue of dog,
> For a charm of powerful trouble,
> Like a hell-broth boil and bubble.
> Scale of dragon, tooth of wolf,
> Witches' mummy, maw and gulf
> Of the ravined salt-sea shark,
> Root of hemlock, digged i'th' dark;
> Make the gruel thick and slab.
> Add therto a tiger's chaudron
> For th'ingredience of our cauldron.
>   Double, double, toil and trouble,
>   Fire burn, and cauldron bubble.
> Cool it with a baboon's blood,
> Then the charm is firm and good.

Shakespeare recommends that you walk around your cauldron. Depending on your kitchen, this can be quite difficult. Do your best.

Filetting a snake can be quite a challenge – your butcher can do this for you. Keep the bones – they can be used as toothpicks.

The woolliest bats are to be found in late autumn.

Scaling a dragon is similar to scaling a fish; hold the dragon head-down in the sink and use the back of a good knife to remove the scales under running water. You can scale the complete dragon and keep the scales for future recipes.

Remember to remove the wolf's tooth before serving!
   The dish can be frozen and kept in the freezer for up to four centuries!

---

32 Anspielung auf *Macbeth* IV,1,4–38.

128   Cooking with Shakespeare

Obviously you will have to begin with the preparation of this dish well in advance!

There is no way of telling if you have actually charmed your pot; it depends on how successful you were at walking around the cauldron with the poisoned entrails – see above.

Keep the frog for the next nine occasions – after all, if you have a good frog, you shouldn't eat it all at once.

Take the dog for a long walk first. The more the dog pants, the easier it will be to remove the tongue.

'Chawdron' is an old word for entrails. Organisations such as the WWF are making it increasingly difficult to find fresh tiger entrails.

The baboon's blood should be kept in the refrigerator for at least half an hour before use, otherwise it will not have the desired cooling effect. A good source of baboon's blood is: www.baboonshop.com/products/entrailsandblood/

1 **potage** (Fr.): Suppe. | 2 **cauldron** ['kɔːldrᵊn]: Kessel. | 3 **entrails**: Eingeweide. | 4 **toad**: Kröte. | 7 **charmèd**: be-, verzaubert. | 8 **fenny**: das Sumpfland bewohnend, Sumpf... | 10 **newt**: Molch. | 14 **scale**: Schuppe. | 15 **mummy**: Mumie(nsaft); galt als Volksheilmittel und wurde zum Balsamieren verwendet; daher auch: balsamiertes Fleisch. | 16 **ravined**: vollgefressen. | 17 **hemlock**: Schierling (giftige Pflanzenart). | 18 **gruel**: Brei. | **slab**: halbfest. | 23 **baboon**: Pavian. | [zu Z. 11] **to pant**: hecheln. | [zu Z. 14] **sink**: Spüle. | [zu Z. 19] **WWF**: Abk. für *World Wide Fund For Nature*, internationale Naturschutzorganisation.

Cooking with Shakespeare 129

Shakespeare in Advertising

The first use of Shakespeare in advertising goes back to the London publisher Jacob Tonson. He used the Chandos portrait as a trademark from 1710 onwards:

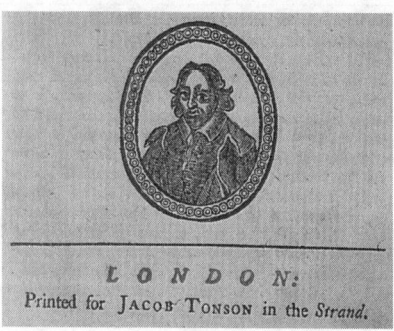

You could say that using Shakespeare to advertise *books* was not very creative, but the advertising industry has made up for these inauspicious beginnings, and since then the Bard and his characters have been used to advertise cigars, cars, computers, beer and all sorts of other things. Possibly the most famous product named after one of Shakespeare's creations is the Cuban "Romeo y Julieta" ci-

---

3 f. **Chandos portrait:** Das als Vorlage genutzte, 552 × 438 mm große Ölgemälde (heute im Besitz der Londoner National Portrait Gallery) ist wohl das einzige zu Lebzeiten (zwischen 1600 und 1610) entstandene Porträt von Shakespeare. Benannt ist es nach dem ehemaligen Eigentümer James Brydges, 3rd Duke of Chandos. Die Identität des Künstlers ist ungewiss. | 4 **from 1710 onwards:** hier: seit 1710. | 7 **inauspicious** [ˌɪnɔːˈspɪʃəs]: ungünstig, nicht vielversprechend.

gar. There are also Hamlet cigars ("Happiness is a cigar called Hamlet" – see p. 136) and Falstaff cigars, but it is the star-crossed lovers who have given their name to perhaps the most famous cigar (or rather: collection of cigars) in the world. Just why a cigar should be named after two unhappy teenagers is a difficult question to answer.

1 **star-crossed lovers:** Anspielung auf die unglücklich Liebenden Romeo und Julia (*Romeo and Juliet*, Prologue, 6), deren Liebe unter keinem guten Stern stand.

Other characters have been used successfully in advertising campaigns, too. Interestingly, advertisers prefer to use tragic figures, such as King Lear and Hamlet, to get their message across. In 1997, King Lear featured in an ad for Coca-Cola. It shows Lear ready to divide up his kingdom. Two of his daughters promise him loyalty, but he chooses the third daughter, who offers him a supply of ice-cold drinks (a very wise choice). Advertisers like to depict Hamlet as a man who knows how to enjoy himself. A major brewery shows him about to meditate on Yorick's skull, but instead of philosophising, Hamlet drops the skull, improvises a

5 **to divide s.th. up:** etwas aufteilen. | 8 **to depict:** darstellen. |
9 **brewery:** Brauerei. | 10 **to meditate on s.th.:** über etwas meditieren, sinnieren. | **skull:** Schädel.

Seven characters in search of seven cars

Prince Hal first! He's got flair! So give him the Corsair. Not just for its flair. But for its princely comfort and royal quality. Cleopatra of course will just have to have a Mk III Zodiac, for the speed, status and luxury that befit a queen. Now! For Romeo-and-Juliet! Only the Capri, that rich jewel of a car. Benedick prefers something smart and snappy — the Anglia. Bravo! For Prospero, the tempestuous magician, something magical. Like the Cortina, which pulls so many big-car qualities out of its small-car costs. What about Falstaff, the mountainous Falstaff. Choose for him a car that makes molehills out of mountains. The Zephyr 4. Or the Zephyr 6 if he needs to make even faster escapes. Shylock has an embarrassment of choice. *Every* Ford car with its outstanding quality, proven reliability and unbeatable value for money, gives him his pound of flesh.

FORD — the dramatic choice

football pass, and is celebrated as a beer drinker who "gets it right". On a slightly different note, John Cleese, in an advertisement for IBM computers, asks himself "to be, or not to be" – but then decides it would be better to ask his computer instead of asking himself. After all, the computer will be able to help him "with all those little everyday domestic problems".

A rare exception to the concentration of the potential customers' attention on one particular character or situation is the remarkable advertisement for the fleet of Ford cars from the 1960s, "seven characters in search of seven cars". If you want to know what sort of car Henry V would have driven, or Romeo and Juliet (who, together, count as just one character), Cleopatra, Benedick, Prospero, Falstaff, or Shylock – then the Ford Motor Company has the answer (see p. 137).

More recently, Google has used the famous 'seven ages of man' speech from *As You Like It* (II,7,139–166) to advertise their Google Plus social networking and identity service – with a baby named William. The speech is edited, and there are only six ages:

JAQUES.   All the world's a stage,
And all the men and women merely players.
They have their exits and their entrances,
And one man in his time plays many parts,
[...]. At first the infant,

---

2 **Cleese:** John C. (geb. 1939), englischer Schauspieler und Schriftsteller. Bekanntheit erlangte er durch die Fernsehserie *Monty Python's Flying Circus* (1969–74). | 23 **player:** Schauspieler.

134 Shakespeare in Advertising

Mewling and puking in the nurse's arms.
Then the whining schoolboy with his satchel
And shining morning face […]
[…]. And then the lover,
Sighing like furnace, with a woeful ballad
[…]. Then, a soldier,
Full of strange oaths, and bearded like the pard,
[…]
Seeking the bubble reputation
Even in the cannon's mouth. And then the justice,
In fair round belly with good capon lin'd,
[…]
Full of wise saws and modern instances;
[…]. The sixth age shifts
Into the lean and slippered pantaloon,
With spectacles on nose and pouch on side,
His youthful hose, well saved, a world so wide
[…].

---

1 **to mewl:** wimmern, winseln, weinen. | **to puke:** spucken, kotzen. | 2 **to whine:** jammern. | **satchel:** Schulranzen. | 5 **furnace:** Schmelzofen. | **woeful:** traurig. | 7 **pard:** Leopard. | 11 **capon** ['keɪpən]: Kapaun. | **lin'd:** gefüllt. | 13 **saws:** Sprüche, Weisheit. | 15 **pantaloon:** Kniehose (galt als typisch für einen alten Mann). | 16 **pouch:** Geldbeutel.

shAkspEr

f U R n a hurry U cn uz yor thumz 2 snd yor fRnz som shAkspEr.[33] mAbE U wnt 2 snd a rOmntc quote 2 yor gf o bf:

> shaL I compR Di 2 a smrz dA?

o do U lIk mrder & deth?:

> iz DIS a dggr whch I c b4 me,
> d h&L 2wRd my h&?

o mAbE U tink Richard III iz gr8:

> nw iz d wNtR of our discntnt
> mAd gloryos sumR by DIS son of Yrk

dEz lines frm 12th nyt R also populR – dey R bout msc & luv:

> if msc b da fd ov luv ply on

do U knO wot plays dEz quotes R frm?

> 2 b, r nt 2 b dat iz d Q
> wthr ts noblr n d mnd 2 sufr

[33] *Sonnet* 18, *Macbeth* II,1,33f., *Richard III* I,1,1f., *Twelth Night* I,1,1, *Hamlet* III,1,58–62, *Macbeth* V,5,18–27, *Romeo and Juliet* II,1,44–48, *Henry V* IV,3,64–67.

d slngs & arowz of outrAjs fortn
r 2 tAk armz agnst a C f trblz,
& by oposn nd em?

2mrw & 2mrw & 2mrw
crEpz n dis pety plAs frm dA 2 dA
2 d lst silabl of rcrdd tIm
& al our ystdAz hv lItd f%lz
d way 2 dsty def. out, out, brief ~=.
LIfs bt a walkin shado, a p%r plAR
dat struts & frets Hs hr upon d stage
& thN iz hErd n mo. tis a tAl
tld by an ejit, ful of snd & fury
sgnfyn nutin.

bt, sft! wot lIt thru yndr wndo brAkz?
Ts d Est, & Juliet iz d sn.
ArIs, fair sn, & kil d envios m%n
hu iz alredi sk & pAl w grEf
dat thou hr mAd art fr mo fair thn she.

& gntlmn n Englnd, nw a-bed
shl fnk thmslvs acrsd dey wr not hr
& hld thr mnh%dz chEp whl NE spk
dat fort w us on St Crspns Da

How to Draw Shakespeare

Follow these simple instructions to produce your own authentic portrait of the Bard. When you are finished, take the portrait to the nearest Shakespeare museum.[34] Say it is an original likeness of the Bard, adding that you discovered in your cellar, or that an old aunt left it to you after she passed away.[35] *Very important*: In order to convince the museum/library/research centre that your portrait is genuine, you must give it a ridiculous name. Tell them you have found the long-lost "Houjlijk portrait", or the "Chaque-y-spir portrait", or the "Braithwaithe-Smitheringale portrait". Remember to ask for cash.

34 Why not try one of the following institutions: The Folger Shakespeare Library, Washington, D.C.; Shakespeare Centre Library, Stratford-upon-Avon; The British Library, London; The National Portrait Gallery, London; The Bodleian Library, Oxford.
35 This is not as unlikely as it might seem. After all, in 2004 a housewife from Stockport, near Manchester in England, received a letter from her solicitor saying that she had inherited a copy of the First Folio edition of Shakespeare's plays. Even though it was damaged, it was sold for over £150,000.

---

5 **likeness:** Bild, Abbild. | 7 **to pass away:** entschlafen. | 8f. **genuine:** echt. | 19 **solicitor:** Rechtsanwalt.

Editorische Notiz

Sämtliche Zitate aus den Werken Shakespeares beziehen sich auf die Ausgabe: William Shakespeare, *The Complete Works*, hrsg. von Stanley Wells, Gary Taylor, John Jowett und William Montgomery, 2. Aufl., Oxford: Oxford University Press, 2005.

Das Glossar erklärt in der Regel alle Wörter, die im *Thematischen Grund- und Aufbauwortschatz Englisch* von Gernot Häublein und Recs Jenkins (Stuttgart: Ernst Klett Sprachen GmbH, 2009) nicht enthalten sind.

Im Glossar verwendete englische Abkürzungen

arch.	archaic (veraltet)
coll.	colloquial (umgangssprachlich)
fig.	figuratively (figurativ, übertragen)
Fr.	French
iron.	ironical
o.s.	oneself
pl.	plural
poet.	poetical (dichterisch, gehoben)
prov.	proverbial (sprichwörtlich)
s.o.	someone
s.th.	something
vulg.	vulgar (vulgär, derb)

Literaturhinweise

Barlow, Patrick, *Shakespeare: The Truth. Or: From Glover to Genius*, London: Methuen, 1983.

Burt, Richard, *Unspeakable ShaXXXspeares. Queer Theory and American Kiddie Culture*, New York: St. Martin's Press, 1998.

Carpenter, Humphrey, *Shakespeare Without the Boring Bits*, London: Viking, 1994.

Cope, Wendy, *Making Cocoa for Kingsley Amis*, London: Faber and Faber, 1986 [u. ö.].

LoMonico, Michael, *The Shakespeare Book of Lists*, Franklin Lakes: New Page Books, 2001.

Kiernan, Pauline, *Filthy Shakespeare. Shakespeare's Most Outrageous Sexual Puns*, London: Quercus, 2006.

Schoenbaum, Marilyn (Hrsg.), *A Shakespeare Merriment. An Anthology of Shakespearean Humor*, New York: Garland, 1988 (Garland Reference Library of the Humanities, 836).

The Shakespeare Revue, compiled by Christopher Luscombe and Malcolm McKee, London: Nick Hern Books, 1994.

Symington, Rodney, *The Nazi Appropriation of Shakespeare. Cultural Politics in the Third Reich*, Lewiston: Edwin Mellen, 2005.

Text- und Abbildungsnachweise

18 Richard Armour: Shakespeare's Life. In: R. A.: Twisted Tales from Shakespeare. New York: McGraw-Hill, 1957. S. 3–6. – Copyright © 1957 by Richard Armour. Reprinted by permission of Geoff Armour, Carlsbad, California.

22 Sam Schoenbaum: Shakespeare's Pubs.* In: S. Sch.: Shakespeare's Lives. New Edition. Oxford: Clarendon Press, 1991. Kap. 2. S. 48 f. – Copyright © S. Schoenbaum 1991. Reprinted by permission of Oxford University Press.

25 A Shakespearean Map of the U.S.A. In: Michael Dobson / Stanley Wells (Hrsg.): The Oxford Companion to Shakespeare. New York: Oxford University Press, 2009. – Copyright © David Jouris / Hold the Mustard Productions.

32 Jürgen Gutsch: Sonnet 18 in Bavarian. (Originaltitel: Sonett 18 in Oberbairisch.) Zuerst in: J. G.: "Millions of strange Shadows" – Vom Übersetzen der Shakespeare-Sonette in jüngerer Zeit (nicht nur) ins Deutsche. In: Shakespeare-Jahrbuch 139 (2003). S. 180. Vom Autor revidierte Fassung. – Abdruck mit Genehmigung des Autors.

32 Hanns Vogel: "All the World's a stage" in Bavarian. (Originaltitel: A Theater is as ganze Lebn – Eine bayerische Variante für unsere Zeit.) In: H. V. (Hrsg.): Ein wenig staad, ein wenig lustig. Sechsundvierzig Geschichten und Gedichte bayerischer und fränkischer Autoren. Dachau: Verlagsanstalt "Bayerland", 1986. S. 21 f. – Copyright © Verlagsanstalt Bayerland, Dachau 1986. Abdruck mit Genehmigung der Verlagsanstalt Bayerland.

41 Zeichnung von Bernard Schoenbaum. In: Marilyn Schoenbaum (Hrsg.): A Shakespeare Merriment. An Anthology of Shakespearean Humor. New York: Garland, 1988. – Copyright © 1985 The New Yorker Magazine, Inc.

49 Zeichnung von Chris Mould. In: Christopher Luscombe / Malcolm McKee (Hrsg.): The Shakespeare Revue. London: Nick Hern Books, 1994.

52 David Crystal / Ben Crystal: Searching for Cyphers. In:

D. C. / B. C.: The Shakespeare Miscellany. London: Penguin, 2005. S. 159. – Copyright © David Crystal and Ben Crystal, 2005. Abdruck mit Genehmigung der Penguin Group, London.

53 Richard Armour: Authorship of the Plays. In: R. A.: Twisted Tales from Shakespeare. New York: McGraw-Hill, 1957. S. 148–151. – Copyright © 1957 by Richard Armour. Reprinted by permission of Geoff Armour, Carlsbad, California.

54 William Shakespeare. His Method of Work. In: Michael Dobson / Stanley Wells (Hrsg.): The Oxford Companion to Shakespeare. New York: Oxford University Press, 2009. – Copyright © Folger Shakespeare Library.

59 Ben Crystal: A Legendary Blues Guitarist.* In: B. C.: Shakespeare on Toast. Getting a Taste for the Bard. Cambridge: Icon Books, 2008. S. 14. – Copyright © 2008 Ben Crystal.

61 Der kleine William liest seiner Familie "an den langen Winterabenden am strahlenden Kaminfeuer vor, denn der Vater sowohl wie die Mutter waren des Lesens nur wenig kundig". Liebig-Reklamebild von 1906. Aus: Ulrich Suerbaum: Der Shakespeare-Führer. Stuttgart: Reclam, 2001.

62 Ian Doescher: William Shakespeare's *Star Wars*. In: I. D.: William Shakespeare's *Star Wars*. Philadelphia: Quirk Books, 2013. S. 8–10. – Copyright © & ™ 2013 Lucasfilm Ltd. All rights reserved. Courtesy of Lucasfilm Ltd.

65 f. Shakespeare's Tragedies – Everybody Dies. Original Concept by Cam Magee. Design by Caitlin S. Griffin. Copyright © National Theatre, South Bank, London SE1 9PX.

67 Richard Curtis: The Skinhead Hamlet. In: John Lloyd / Sean Hardie (Hrsg.): Not 1982: Not the Nine O'Clock News Rip-Off Annual. London: Faber and Faber, 1981. Zit. nach: Simon Brett (Hrsg.): The Faber Book of Parodies. London. Faber and Faber, 1984. S. 316–320.

74 Desmond Olivier Dingle: The Famed "To Be or Not To Be" Scene from *Hamlet*. A modern verse rendition. In: Patrick Barlow: Shakespeare: The Truth or From Glover to Genius. London: Methuen, 1993. S. 182–184. – Copyright © 1993 by Patrick Barlow.

75 John Philip Kemble (1757–1823) als Hamlet. Ölgemälde (1801) von Sir Thomas Lawrence (1769–1830). London: Tate Gallery.

76 Sir Arthur Quiller-Couch: A Soliloquy Simplified: "To be, or the Contrary"?* In: A. Qu.-C.: On the Art of Writing. (1916.) Cambridge: Cambridge University Press, 2008. Kap. 5: Interlude: On Jargon. S. 84 f. – Copyright © Cambridge University Press 1916.

77 Desmond Olivier Dingle: The Tragedy of *Othello*. A modern verse rendition. In: Patrick Barlow: Shakespeare: The Truth or From Glover to Genius. London: Methuen, 1993. S. 175–178. – Copyright © 1993 by Patrick Barlow.

81 Shakespeare According to Gyles Brandreth.* Aus: Gyles Brandreth: Long Live the Lipogram. In: G. B.: The Joy of Lex. New York: Quill, 1983. S. 62 f. – Copyright © 1987 Gyles Brandreth.

85 James Thurber: The Macbeth Murder Mystery. In: J. Th.: My World – And Welcome To It. New York: Harcourt, Brace and Company, 1942. S. 33–39. – Copyright © 1942 by James Thurber, copyright renewed © 1970 by Helen W. Thurber and Rosemary Thurber Sauers. Reprinted by permission of Houghton Mifflin Harcourt Publishing Company. All rights reserved.

92 Humphrey Carpenter: *The Merchant of Venice*, told by Lancelot Gobbo, Shylock's Servant. In: H. C.: Shakespeare Without the Boring Bits. London: Viking, 1994. S. 54–66. – Copyright © Humphrey Carpenter 1994. Reprinted by permission of Cecily Ware Literary Agents, London.

100 f. Wendy Cope: The Sonnets I and II. From: *Strugnell's Sonnets*. In: W. C.: Making Cocoa for Kingsley Amis. London: Faber and Faber, 1986. S. 56 f. – Copyright © Wendy Cope, 1986.

102 Nick Nicholas: Sonnet 18 (in Klingon). In: N. N.: Selection of Shakespearean Sonnets. http://www.khemorex-klinzhai.de/Hol/kli/sonnets – Copyright © 1994 KLI.

114 Patrick Barlow: The Verse Problem – And How to Master It. In: P. B.: Shakespeare: The Truth or From Glover to Genius. London: Methuen, 1993. S. 149 f. – Copyright © 1993 by Patrick Barlow.

115 Stephen Fry / Hugh Laurie: Shakespeare Masterclass. In: Christopher Luscombe / Malcolm McKee (Hrsg.): The Shakespeare Revue. London: Nick Hern Books, 1994, S. 24 f.

118 Derek Nimmo: A Tale of Revenge from *Macbeth*.* In: D. N.: As the Actress Said to the Bishop. New York: Hodder and Stoughton, 1989. Kap. 1: Early Days. S. 21. – Copyright © 1989 Derek Nimmo.

120, 121, 122 Questions by Richard Armour. In: R. A.: Twisted Tales from Shakespeare. New York: McGraw-Hill, 1957. S. 142, 42, 63 f. – Copyright © 1957 by Richard Armour. Reprinted by permission of Geoff Armour, Carlsbad, California.

123 Patrick Barlow: Shakespeare's Age. In: P. B.: Shakespeare: The Truth or From Glover to Genius. London: Methuen, 1993. S. 29. – Copyright © 1993 by Patrick Barlow.

127 "More newts – Macbeth is staying to dinner!" Zeichnung von Michael ffolkes (d. i. Brian Davis). In: Christopher Luscombe / Malcolm McKee (Hrsg.): The Shakespeare Revue. London: Nick Hern Books, 1994.

130 Verlagslogo nach dem sogenannten "Chandos Portrait". Aus: The Dramatick Works of John Dryden, Esq. London: J. Tonson, 1735. (München: Bayerische Staatsbibliothek.)

131 Zigarrenwerbung "Romeo y Julieta". http://www.habanos.com/images/app/extras/4.-Romeo-y-Julieta-Petit-Churchills-comp.jpg

132 "Happiness is a cigar called Hamlet". Reklame aus dem Jahr 1966. http://vintage-adverts.com/epages/BT3325.sf/en_GB/?ObjectPath=/Shops/BT3325/Products/0001CT&ViewAction=ViewProduct

133 Autowerbung "Seven characters in search of seven cars". In: Michael Dobson / Stanley Wells (Hrsg.): The Oxford Companion to Shakespeare. New York: Oxford University Press, 2009. S. 4.

139 Zeichnung von Rosalie Kletzander (Originalbeitrag).

* Mit einem Sternchen versehene Titel stammen vom Herausgeber des vorliegenden Bandes.

Der Verlag Philipp Reclam jun. dankt für die Nachdruckgenehmigung den Rechteinhabern, die durch den Quellennachweis oder einen folgenden Copyrightvermerk bezeichnet sind. In einigen Fällen waren die Inhaber der Rechte nicht festzustellen. Hier ist der Verlag bereit, nach Anforderung rechtmäßige Ansprüche abzugelten.